UNDERWAY

Reflections on Everyday Grace

UNDERWAY

Reflections on Everyday Grace

By
Elise Seyfried

Copyright © 2011, Elise Seyfried

ISBN 978-1-105-18433-8

Scripture quotations are from New Revised Standard Version Bible © 1989 National Council of Churches of Christ in the United States of America. Used by permission. All rights reserved.

The following essays originally appeared in The Chestnut Hill Local:

Company
De Colores
Picking Battles
Shades of Gray
Skin Deep
Stranger in Paradise
Suppertime
The Luckiest
You've Got a Friend
Underway

Thumper originally appeared in Metropolis.

INTRODUCTION

Underway: adv. & adj.—Already commenced or initiated; in progress. (Nautical) Neither anchored nor moored to a fixed object.

Introductions are so much easier when it's your first book! You can give your name, your background, your inspiration for writing—and it's all brand-new to the reader. By the second time around, veterans of Book #1 prefer that you just cut to the chase. But then there are the others (welcome!!) who are reading Book #2 first…they, justifiably, are curious about writer and reasons.

Soooo…condensed version: I work at a Lutheran church outside of Philadelphia. I've been writing these essays about my funny, crazy life for years. I have a saint of a husband and five terrific children. I write about said church, husband, and children in the essays. I also look for the traces of God's grace in every story, because it's that grace that gets me through. That's it in a nutshell.

I invite you to pick up this book when you're looking for a short reflection or two, especially when you're feeling nervous and insecure—because you'll find a soul mate in nervous, insecure me. We are, all of us, on this journey together. Sometimes, the way ahead is clear as sunrise over the ocean. Often, it's clear as mud. So we need each other, to hold hands and forge ahead anyway. Laugh when we can. Trust that we are living out a plan for our lives, designed by the One who loves us most.

The essays are not chronological, so Steve, the kids and I age irregularly. I'd update everything except that I really love reading that I'm still 48 (helps me forget that I'm 54 now). The messages, hopefully, will speak to you, whatever your age.

All my love and thanks to the amazing friends and family who have stuck with me through the journey that was *Underway*. I can't imagine any travelers, anywhere, with whom I'd rather be.

TABLE OF CONTENTS

Underway 1
Skin Deep 5
Mixed Marriage 9
The Finish Line 13
Company 15
Mannerly 19
Let There Be Light 21
City Girl 25
Great Expectations 29
Music Music Music 33
My Bucket List 37
Electable 41
De Colores 45
Holy Horror 49
Plenty 53
Taking Flight 57
Thumper 61
Still a Few Bugs in the System 65
Shades of Gray 69
Suppertime 73
Found in Translation 77

Picking Battles 81

Rebel with a Cause 85

Going Jesus 89

Letter from Elise 93

Speechless 97

How Glory Goes 101

Join Me 103

Golden Silence 105

What's in a Name? 107

Baby Sister 111

Deconstructing Thanksgiving 115

Gone Fishin' 119

Halfway Home 123

Busy Bee 127

A Novel Idea 131

Blessed Be the Ties that Bind 135

Stranger in Paradise 137

If the Shoe Fits 141

Summer Training 143

You've Got a Friend 147

The Luckiest 151

And the Greatest of These Is Love 155

UNDERWAY

"The best way to keep children at home is to make the home a pleasant atmosphere and let the air out of the tires."

--Dorothy Parker

As with so many other aspects of my life, I have a love/hate relationship with the ocean. I adore sunrises over the sea, sitting at water's edge with a good book, "swimming" (my definition: wading out, ever-so-tentatively, until I am maaaayybee knee-deep in the drink, then scampering smartly ashore at the first hint of an actual wave). But I fear the ocean's power, its depth, its general…wateriness. Since every one of our children's summers has revolved around the Delaware seashore, you can imagine my pretend good cheer, and genuine heart-sinking sensation, each time the kids caroled, "Let's go in!" When they got past the age when I absolutely had to let go of my death grip on their hands (it's been about two or three years now), I had to content myself to watch as they rode in on the tide on their flimsy boogie boards, or jumped— worse, ducked under— the terrifying swells. I would read the same sentence in my book 47 times as my eyes darted, up over the page and out towards my cavorting offspring. Only twice did I actually have reason to be this panicky. Evan was once carried out by a riptide—and promptly rescued by a lifeguard; Julie got a mild concussion by being knocked over in the surf. The other 1800 trips to the beach, the biggest mishaps involved sunscreen in the eyes and sandwiches snatched by ravenous seagulls.

   Well, now my worst sea-related nightmare—being trapped underwater—is currently being lived out by Lt. JG Evan Seyfried, USS Greeneville. Evan is underway, to parts and for times unknown, and I am left, ashore and forlorn, to imagine how I could possibly have mothered a child so totally unfazed by life on a submarine. I'm learning to cope with waiting for whatever news he can share (email, surprisingly, does travel back and forth, but at a virtual snail's pace), hanging on to Evan's reassurance that subs have come a little ways since the small, super-cramped boats featured in WWII movies. I try hard to begin and end the day in prayer for him—prayer for his safety—and then trust in it: let God be God and care for my child where I cannot follow. But still...

Other places I cannot go, now that ALL the Seyfried kids are "underway," one way or another, include the classes Sheridan is teaching at the Curtis Institute. How I'd love to sneak in and listen to my son instruct a roomful of gifted young musicians! But guess what? That invitation has not yet been issued! How about a visit to Rosie's "flat" in London last summer, as she worked on a sound installation for the Royal Opera House? Heck, how about Rosie's front stoop in Boston, hanging out with her Berklee buds? Haven't gotten that invite either!

To finish the roll call, PJ has yet to ask me to a Friday night Millersville University party (I'm sure he probably just lost my phone number), and when Jules has high school friends over, her "special request" is for me to please find something to do in a galaxy far, far away.

So when did I become so darned dispensable? Why does it seem that the clichéd "roots and wings" line is being altered around here, with the roots uprooted and all the wings flapping wildly, propelling them farther and farther from me? I guess I didn't think I'd feel quite so marginalized until I was a good bit older (say, age 126 or so). The other day we had one of those bizarre conversations that seem to be a staple of the Seyfried house. Julie asked who had been scheduled to "get" the brood if anything happened to Steve and me. I responded, "Aunt C." My sister deserves her crown in Heaven for having agreed to this plan (though at the time I am SURE her every prayer was that she be spared life as "Auntie Mom" to five children under age ten). Julie then said, casually, "Well, you know, we'd be fine on our own now, if anything happened. We'd figure it out." What should have been a reassuring comment, instead triggered an unreasonable longing to turn back the hands of time to the anxious, crazy, exhausting days when I was capital N Needed.

Oh I know, I know, they still need me, just in a different way. Their independence and competence are such positive things, qualities they have worked hard to develop and deserve to enjoy.

And I truly believe that I am still on speed dial when life's crises hit. And I really never want to become Clingy Mother, demanding hourly check-ins from her little ones.

So, where does that leave me? Redefining myself, for sure. But maybe that's something I really needed to do. Like it or not, I am "underway" as well. Setting sail on that ocean I both love and hate, that ocean called life: a new kind of mom, onward to the next adventure.

SKIN DEEP

"For by the grace given to me I say to everyone among you not to think of yourself more highly than you ought to think, but to think with sober judgment, each according to the measure of faith that God has assigned."

--Romans 12:3

About seven years ago, I chaperoned an elementary school trip to Robbins Park Nature Center with Julie's class. After a hike to Creepy Pond and a look at various shrubs and seedlings outdoors, we went into the cabin where the hands-on science projects were housed. Today's lesson involved a special, super-duper microscope. The images could be projected onto a screen on the wall. The instructor showed us items such as a translucent moth wing and a slice of oak tree bark, magnified hundreds of times. We oohed and aahed at the minute details unveiled. Then came the question: "May we have a volunteer mom to help us out for a minute?" Never one to heed internal warning signals, I stepped forward. "Great! Mrs. Seyfried, will you please place your hand under the microscope?" Uh-oh… ummm…oh well, how bad could it be? A hand is a hand, right? Well, the oohs and aahs were magnified hundreds of times as the children and adults got a gander at my epidermis. Surely there was a mistake. Someone had slipped an old snakeskin under the lens instead! But no, it was me, in living color. The back of my hand was a veritable Grand Canyon of wrinkled skin and sun-damaged cells and age spots. My youthful and dewy flesh (an illusion, granted, born of my poor eyesight and very few mirrors in my house) was gone. There, in its place, was my 95-year-old Grandma's hand! Curse you, super-duper microscope!

    As a little girl, I spent much of each summer frolicking on the sand at Normandy Beach, NJ. Or rather, I spent the first day frolicking and the next weeks recovering from my massive sunburn.

When other children slept like angels after a day in the great outdoors, I was in much too much pain to doze off. "Warm" memories of those July evenings feature my mom soaking a towel in vinegar and applying it to my crimson back. Vinegar was supposed to absorb heat, and it seemed to work—within seconds the towel was so scalding hot that Mom needed to remove it with spaghetti tongs.

For a relatively intelligent person, my IQ plummeted when it came to Sun Sense. As I grew older, I continued to cook myself in the noonday heat, turning over every few minutes like a roasting chicken. And, just like said poultry, I was coated with oil for maximum crispiness. I pitied the friends who wore hats and sat under umbrellas and sported pale complexions year-round. They looked downright sickly! Far better to TAN! Never mind that my snow-white Irish skin wouldn't have turned brown in a jillion years. I would become a bronze goddess or die trying!

Alas, we reap what we sow. All the retinol and "age-defying" lotions and potions in the world haven't made a dent in undoing my decades of self-inflicted skin damage. Mom endured four bouts of malignant melanoma, attributed to her own youthful sun worshipping. So far I have dodged this bullet. Or so I assume—I stay far away from the dermatologist, preferring blissful ignorance as long as possible.

I like to think that my stupidity is only skin deep, that underneath I am a creature of great common sense and wisdom. The baby-faced me inside knows so much better than to make self-destructive choices. The real Elise always does the right thing. I take good care of my body and soul, and I don't try to be something I'm not. Dig down beneath my surface and you will find a gem.

But there's a little problem with this perception. Exactly how far down does one have to go to see this wonderful person? An inch? A mile? How many "superficial" problems do we have to ignore to see my real good nature?

The microscope sees far more clearly than any human eye. It magnifies what is really there, and exposes the often-painful truth. I saw my actual skin under a powerful lens that day at Robbins Park. It was impossible to escape the reality: I am damaged. And largely through my own fault. If I am indeed different, and better, inside, it sure doesn't show.

So is there any hope?

I think, I pray, that there is. The first step is facing the music. Until I acknowledge that my foolish choices are not only skin-deep—that indeed they go right to the bone—nothing will change. I need to acknowledge my deeply-rooted selfishness, my short-sightedness, my carelessness, the "burns" that hurt not only me, but also those I love. I need to examine every inch of me with that super-duper microscope, without making any more excuses. Some irreparable harm has been done, for sure, but as long as there is life there IS hope for improvement.

The view of the shoreline from under an umbrella is just as lovely as it is from under the sun. May I learn to sit there calmly, sink down to my core, and work on improving my innermost self. In the cool of the shade, maybe the healing can finally begin.

MIXED MARRIAGE

Q: What does a mother-in-law call her broom?
A: Basic transportation.

--Anonymous Comedian

Even those of us who are severely joke-challenged probably could recite at least one mother-in-law joke. They usually revolve around her very difficult personality, and the punch lines are always sympathetic to the one ill-treated by "the old battle-axe."

As my own offspring approach the marrying years, I often think about my relationships with future brides and grooms, and I'm guessing Steve does too. My hope is that our feelings will only be fond when The Right One finally comes along for each of the kids.

But what will they, the spouses, think of us? We are sure to be different from them, and their own parents, in many ways. The in-law relationship is a big adjustment for all concerned. From housekeeping habits to child rearing philosophies, there are endless possibilities for misunderstanding and conflict.

I've had my own parents and in-laws on my mind recently. It has been nearly five years since my mother died. Steve's folks have been gone more than 26 years (our children never knew them at all). Our parents were the two most unlike couples I could imagine, a true study in contrasts. How they produced two compatible people remains one of life's mysteries.

My mom grew up wealthy in Westchester County, New York. My dad was an only child. Mom considered emptying the ashtrays to be a thorough room cleaning. Dad's sales career could be compared to that of a less-successful Willy Loman.

Steve's parents, on the other hand, grew up knowing hard times, and came from large families, each one of ten children. Leona was such a demon neatnik that she IRONED THE SHEETS (still in shock over that one). And Phil retired comfortably after a very long career with one firm.

But the differences ran deeper. In my house, a day without an argument was like a day without sunshine. We battled over everything and nothing (mostly nothing). While we always kissed and made up at the end, the next dust-up was never far away. Mom, in particular, was a verbal Muhammad Ali, always knowing just where to jab to score the knockout, and I learned from the best.

In contrast, Steve's childhood could have been an 18-year-long episode of *Ozzie and Harriet.* He had four siblings (the lineup was telegenic: girl, boy, girl, boy, girl), plus an extended family that boasted 65 first cousins. A cross word was Rarely Spoken. Actual fighting was Just Not Done. Even in times of disappointment, such as young Jean Marie's elopement and Steve's decision to leave the seminary, gentle tones and stiff upper lips always prevailed. At Steve's, plates were for food, not for throwing at walls. Guests were always welcome; some, like Cousin Bill, stayed for years. Evenings were spent companionably playing euchre, Indiana's premiere card game.

Needless to say, we both had a rocky beginning with our in-laws. Steve had to learn that Cunninghams hated impromptu company, and that not knocking before entering our house was a federal offense (we needed those frantic seconds to shove the scattered newspapers and soda cans under the sofa). I had to come to terms with Tupperware: every Seyfried leftover was methodically doled into a specific, labeled container for storage. Hey, where was the fun of rooting through the fridge, discovering science experiments that had once been dinner? What's more, the two of us were incomprehensible to each other's parents. I was the too-young, high-falutin' fiancée from Big Bad New York City. Steve was the easygoing guy from the sticks who hated to fight. What was wrong with him?

Steve and I wed. We started to perform in dinner theatre, and all four in-laws loyally attended when they could. Whenever I got a role in a sub-par play, my parents Joan and Tom would gleefully pan the show, saving their accolades for higher quality offerings. Conversely, Steve's parents would ALWAYS gush aloud, "Stevie, that's the best thing you've ever done!!!" They said this after his genuinely impressive star turn in a production of *Cyrano de Bergerac.* They said the exact same thing, to Steve's dismay, after the curtain fell on the excruciating *Not with MY Daughter*!

Eventually we moved to Philadelphia, leaving Mom and Dad in Atlanta, and Leona and Phil in Valdosta, Georgia. Distance worked its magic. Everyone tried hard during visits, but what really worked was the magic of time. Over the years, Steve grew to genuinely love my parents (and, fortunately or unfortunately, learned how to argue quite well, thank you). I came to find his homespun folks much more endearing than annoying.

And now they are gone, all four. And now I understand—being an in-law is no joke. It's the marriage of two families. It's a lifelong series of compromises and accommodations—and revelations too. It's learning to embrace the "other," and see the value in different values. It's—well, it's a lot like life as it should be lived.

God expects His children, all His children, to get along. We come from various places: New York. Valdosta. South Africa. Northern Ireland. Israel. Palestine. We speak different languages, literally or figuratively. We iron our sheets or we don't, so to speak. We need to recognize that we are a family, a blended family—mine and yours. None of us perfect, but all us lovable to our Parent. A Parent who just wants to see us start loving each other.

And when that day finally comes, He will, unreservedly, say, "That's the best thing you've ever done."

THE FINISH LINE

"There are two kinds of people: those who finish what they start, and so on..."

--Robert Byrne

Aside from other people's sentences, I am not a great finisher. I still have my singular attempt at knitting: the beginnings of a scarf. It is a rather grotesque length of bright orange yarn, which I attacked with gusto and a rampant disregard for such things as stitches (I learned later you should count them) and pattern (you should have one). I always leave food on my plate and running shoes gathering dust in the corner of my closet. My piano lessons ended, diminuendo, as gradually Sheridan and I both gave up on me.

Other things I have yet to finish include my Irish language tapes. The sum total of my linguistic prowess: I can say "God bless the cow" in Gaelic when handed a glass of milk—a particularly useful feat for someone who'll probably never get to the Emerald Isle, and doesn't like milk if she does. And another thing—I've never come close to completing any exercise class I've ever taken. I'm especially good at dropping the ones that cost the most money; the only part of me that loses weight is my wallet.

The "starts" are boffo. I just wish I could keep my wild initial enthusiasm going. Perhaps it's my attention span, or lack thereof. I prefer to think that relationships, not tasks or skills, are my priorities. Quitter? Not me! But the evidence keeps piling up… the bedroom that has been ¾ painted for ten years… the books I've been promising Sheridan I would read… the laughably unfinished "to do" lists. My sister Maureen was my equal in this department. It got to the point that she would write down "wake up," so that she could cross off SOMEthing that day. My other sister, Carolyn, however, puts me and Mo to shame. Carolyn is great on relationships AND has the tasks-and-skills thing down too (so there goes my excuse).

My current church job encourages a certain amount of completion. Vacation Bible School has an end, as well as a beginning. Eventually the mission trip is over and we go home. But even at church, testimony to my flightiness is everywhere. The neatly-kept Sunday School scrapbooks from 2002-2008, with absolutely nothing done since. The move to my new office—months later, my energy and interest in the relocation process have totally petered out. I still have stuff (some of it maybe important?) in Office #1, and probably always will.

Faith can peter out, too; in fact, that's often how it's lost. Not the big dramatic moment, but the gradual loss of interest and enthusiasm. We quit going to church. We quit reading Scripture. We quit praying. We come to feel we can handle life just fine without God's input, thank you very much. He is relegated to the bottom of our "to do" list, the place we don't bother getting around to. We start out with a bang: that clear and beautiful acceptance of the Divine Reality that four-year-olds have. But we all too frequently end with a whimper, a lifetime down the road. What should be, as St. Paul describes, a spirited race with a glorious finish line in sight becomes a weary trudge towards the conclusion of our earthly time, as we flat out give up hope of anything better coming along.

But here's something to remember. God is no quitter. We are His precious works of art and He still works on us daily, never losing interest, never giving up. He runs the race beside us and cheers us on. He tries to remind us that we'd be happier if we could only trust in Him. He urges us to see the world as an ongoing, exhilarating adventure and, when we just can't, He offers us a place to go with our sorrows—to Him. And He has Paradise waiting for us all at the end, whether we finish early or late.

I was going to go for funny and end this in mid-sentence, but instead I think I'll do what I so infrequently manage to do in life. I'll finish. It's never too late to find those knitting needles again, to speak that new language, to take on new challenges and see them all the way through. I'll try to pick up my feet and run now. I'll get back in that "spirited race." And it may not be too late for me to finish strong.

COMPANY

"We labor to make a house a home, then every time we're expecting visitors, we rush to turn it back into a house."

--Robert Brault

Is mine the only house on earth that spontaneously bursts into Cobweb Central when company is coming?

    I swear, I can have thoroughly cleaned every square inch of my home sweet home MINUTES earlier, and am relaxing, admiring the polished and scrubbed fruit of my labors. But then the phone rings, heralding the impending arrival of guests. In the blink of an eye, a thick layer of dirt drifts in and settles on everything from lampshades to floorboards. The kitchen floor suddenly oozes grime. The bathrooms, which mere moments before were hotel-worthy, now qualify as toxic zones. The hair on the carpet makes it look like we own a giant shedding dog, when in reality our lone pet swims in a bowl, guiltless. So I swing into my most delightful persona, Maid from Hell. Beware, husband and children! Brooms will be flung at you, scrub buckets will soar in your direction! I will develop octopus arms as I attempt to sanitize the microwave, refrigerator, dishwasher and family room carpet, while washing the shower curtain and re-pointing the chimney, all at the same time. As the doomsday clock continues its relentless ticking, I decide it's time to paint the dining room ceiling, re-seal the back deck and iron the drapes. By the time the company is due to arrive, I am sprawled in a chair, waving the limp dustcloth of defeat, totally spent.

    And that doesn't include shopping for, and then preparing, the party food. What my menu lacks in "luxe" due to our austere budget, it must make up in "clever." So it's handmade naan bread, hand-dipped chocolate strawberries, hand-crafted cheese puffs. Take a peek at the site of Seyfried's Kitchen Kapers and you will probably not be struck by its resemblance to the super-organized mise-en-place of *Top Chef*. You probably will be struck by the fine coating of flour on everything, including the cook. And the chaos. You'll definitely notice the chaos. Burned fingers, broken glass…my specialties!

Lest you think I exaggerate, ask any one of my children to imitate me in full-guest-alert mode. You will get quite the eyeful and earful, believe me. They really have my number, and it's not a number anyone would want to dial.

The more I fuss and plan, the bigger my parties seem to flop, too. For years, we invited the neighborhood for a Christmas weekend open house, which of course annually ruined Christmas Day itself, because all of my focus was on the mega-event to come. The final year of our big "do," a wicked virus spread through town. I had prepped food for 60 people. By 10 AM on the Big Day, 45 people had called in sick. We were stuck eating the ton of festive crackers and dip until we, too, felt quite, quite ill.

I don't have the energy to entertain often, given my absurd standards of hostess perfection. And it's a shame, because I want to. Really. Hospitality is a spiritual practice to which I am honestly drawn. On those rare occasions that either a) I am still in shape to appreciate my company when they come or b) I am caught by surprise and have no choice but to relax and welcome visitors without the manic prep time, I genuinely enjoy being with people.

Why do I assume everyone will cross my threshold sporting white gloves, ready to tsk-tsk? Do I subject my host or hostess' homes to this laser-beam scrutiny? Of course not—I am so unobservant that I would not notice the sudden addition of an in-ground pool in their living room, or a wayward tree growing through their kitchen window since my last visit. If I registered a little speck on the floor or dust mote on the windowsill, I would only feel more comfortable, not less. So why do I give no credit to my friends?

If Jesus gave me a buzz and said he'd be swinging by for dinner this evening, do I honestly think He'd give a darn if my screen door latch was still broken and my cheese puffs lacked sufficient puffiness?

As the holidays arrive, may I try to be a little more Mary and a whole lot less Martha (both biblical and Stewart). May I cherish my loved ones and fling my door open wide to welcome them (and without the latch that should be easy). May I do the best I can to get ready, and then let the rest go. It's the togetherness that matters, sharing the time of our lives.

But I hear dim lights and candles cover a multitude of sins.

MANNERLY

"A man's manners are a mirror in which he shows his portrait."

--Goethe

My schedule is rather hectic these days, and so, as I gulp my morning java, I only have time to peruse the highlights in *The Philadelphia Inquirer*. Of course, these highlights include my horoscope, the strangely riveting comic strip "Rex Morgan," and, most of all, the advice column. I am particularly addicted to the latter, a never-ending parade of gaffes and faux pas followed by crisp, common-sense responses. Question: "May I ask my wedding guests for cash to fund my dream honeymoon to Fiji?" Answer: "Are you kidding?" Question: "My neighbor drops off her six kids every morning for me to watch before school, even when they're sick. She never thanks me or offers to pay. Should I say something?" Answer: "Are you kidding?" Question: "My mother-in-law…" Answer: "Are you kidding?"

What's up, people? We humans seem to be operating with a <u>serious</u> manners deficit these days. We interrupt; we cut each other off in traffic; we push and shove to get our way. Debates have devolved into screaming matches. And the disrespect we have for one another carries over to disrespect for the environment, from cigarette butts flipped out of car windows, to paper cups and sandwich wrappers thrown on the grass in the park.

My mom was my standard bearer for trying to do and say the right thing. She used to write thank you notes to people to thank them for sending her thank you notes—I'm dead serious. No crime in our house was more egregious than hurting each other's feelings. Were she here today, she would be taking just about everyone to task. I can hear Joanie now: *No, politicians on both sides of the aisle, it is actually <u>not</u> all right to make up horrific lies about each* *other to win elections. Hey, Charlie Cell Phone, it is extremely rude to kill people on the Blue Route because you can't wait 10 minutes to make that business call. Um, excuse me, ma'am, but 27 cans of creamed corn do not count as one item in the express lane.*

When our kids were little, we tried to take a page from the Grandma Joanie book, and insisted on decent treatment, for ourselves and those around us. Even at a young age, the children noticed the friends who were, and were not, similarly encouraged. We still laugh about a friend of Sheridan's who got a ride home with us from school one afternoon. When we reached his house, the boy leapt out of the car. He paused, searching his memory bank for an appropriate parting comment ("thank you," perhaps?) Finally, out came "Alrighty, then!" Bottom line: I don't think it scarred my gang indelibly to say "please," to wait their turn, to hold doors, and to give up their seats to older people.

Now, I don't advocate going back to the Victorian era, when etiquette was ridiculously complex, and a misplaced salt spoon (yes, they had salt spoons) on the dinner table was a gasp-worthy breach. But our society seems to have thrown Baby Miss Manners out with the bathwater, and jettisoned common courtesy entirely. And it's not just Americans. Julie was visiting Rosie in London this summer and they shopped at the popular emporium Primark. The girls were appalled at the throng of bargain hunters who literally grabbed things out of other people's shopping carts.

We have only one month that includes a national gratitude holiday, November. Moving forward, wouldn't it be wonderful to make <u>each</u> month truly a month for gratitude? For loving kindness? For plain old good manners? Manners require noticing those around us not as obstacles to push aside, but as fellow travelers on this planet. Being polite should not be seen as a sign of weakness—far from it.

What a world we'd have if it was OK, even cool, to be thoughtful again.

And yes, Kanye West, I'm talking to you too.

LET THERE BE LIGHT

"I have come into the world as a light, so that no one who believes in me should stay in darkness."

--John 12:46

Hi. I'm Elise, and I am a Lightaholic.

It's a painful thing to be in December.

Give me sunlight, moonlight, starlight, candlelight, firelight, flashlights, footlights, even florescent lights…I love 'em all. Even if it were possible to illuminate my life with all of the above simultaneously, it still wouldn't totally satisfy my light cravings. Light beer notwithstanding, there is little labeled "light" that I do not adore. I have a desk lamp at work equipped with a special light bulb that imitates outdoor lighting, designed especially for those afflicted with Seasonal Affective Disorder (moi), given to me by my good friend Mary Ellen. It is on every single solitary second I'm at my desk. Thomas Edison: My Ultimate Hero. When at home, Steve and I do the (maybe familiar?) Dance of the Spouses: I flit from room to room flipping "on" switches; Mr. Cheapo follows close behind, turning them off. Repeat ad nauseum. (Btw, this Dance is also done with our thermostat.)

So what do I have against the dark? Velvety, mysterious, haunting, romantic…dark is nice, right?

Not for me. My dreams (and my dreams would make Stephen King blanch) are all set shrouded in gloom, embedded in bottomless blackness. My night driving skills are just about nil (even with glasses, Point A to Point B after sunset is a real crapshoot). I hate evening strolls, because, even though my outerwear is lit up like a Christmas tree, I am convinced I will be mowed down by a reckless motorist, or attacked by an invisible animal—perhaps a rabid chipmunk? Even as a child, Halloween was a source of definite mixed feelings…would the prospect of collecting a mother lode of sugar trump my terror of the day's closing hours?

Summer, needless to say, is absolutely my time to shine. Indeed, the (no pun intended) highlight of our mission trip to Alaska was the 18 hours of "day." The wintertime, early descent of night brings a corresponding descent of my spirits. If I could get away with jammies at supper and beddy-byes immediately after, you can bet I would. Why should hibernation be wasted on the bears?

When the kids were little and afraid of the dark, I left the door open and the nightlight burning. If they needed to, I let them sleep with a bedside lamp on. I understood, on a primal level, their fear of not being seen, of not being able to see. Apples plunking down right beside the maternal tree, they had a variety of nocturnal issues, from night terrors to sleepwalking to the general "creeps." I remember the night PJ made us take all the *Goosebumps* books out of the room the three boys shared, because the rather graphic book covers scared him so. Each and every time, the very act of turning on a light soothed them, calmed them, banished their demons.

Which is why every Biblical reference to Christ as the Light of the World resonates so, so deeply with me. I need the light, every minute of the day. Even when I do my painful daily pass at the mirror (oh come ON, Mother Nature, another wrinkle? Really?) I am grateful for the light that makes my vision possible. Light to me is warmth, is joy, is safety. And when Jesus calls me to be a light as well, I am inspired to try to be just that...a source of warmth, joy and safety for others. To help banish their demons. To illuminate their paths. To brighten their spirits.

Sometimes we are the children crying out for light. Sometimes we are the grownups, flipping the "on" switch. Life affords us many chances to play both roles

The forces of darkness are much on my mind these days, as wars drag interminably on and human suffering seems to be on the daily increase. Try as we might to wish it away, Evil exists in this world. We as people are gifted with choices, every minute of the day: we can stand up to Evil and, with God, defeat it, or we can let it creep into our lives like a black cloud creeps over and blocks the sun.

Remember that moment at the end of rock concerts years ago? Maybe they still do this—it's been a little while for me. In a darkened and cavernous hall, individual cigarette lighters would be ignited and suddenly the whole vast room would change. The raucous circus-like atmosphere would become, almost, a holy place, where everyone's flickering flame counted, added to the whole, mattered. Bathed everything and everyone in a new kind of light. Declared brave victory over the night.

As we inch, infinitesimally, towards Spring, I pray that we relish our light, in all its forms. I pray that we use that light to see our Lord in every face, in every corner of our world. And I pray, always, for a brighter morning. For all of us.

CITY GIRL

"The kiss of the sun for pardon/The song of the birds for mirth/One is nearer God's heart in a garden/ Than anywhere else on earth."

--Dorothy Frances Gurney

Wow, does that mean the place closest to my heart is farthest from the Almighty's?

I was born in Greenwich Village and lived in the behemoth Stuyvesant Town complex on the Lower East Side of New York City. As a little girl, I thought everybody went to sleep to the sounds of screeching taxicab brakes, relentless car horns and the occasional gunshot. I assumed everyone's school bus was filled with adult commuters, and plastered with ads for Seagram's whiskey and Marlboro cigarettes. I was used to impatient sales clerks and gruff deli owners and graffiti-bedecked playgrounds. In the summers, when we trekked to the Jersey Shore for vacation, I truly believed every state demarcation looked like the printed New York/New Jersey line inside the Holland Tunnel. The first movie I saw away from Radio City Music Hall left me perplexed. Didn't those dancing Rockettes accompany every film, everywhere? Aside from pigeons, and the tiny, ridiculously beribboned and pampered dogs prancing on leashes beside their owners along Fifth Avenue, the only animals I ever saw resided in the Central Park Zoo.

Mine was the myopia of the die-hard urban dweller—I compared every out-of-city experience to my life as a Manhattanite (and found most all of them wanting).

I LOVED New York. Still do love cities—every sooty, smelly, exciting inch of them.

And even though my life's journey has taken me far, far away from the hustle-bustle of the metropolitan scene, I remain a city girl. Oh, don't get me wrong. I enjoy a nice bed of roses as much as the next person—I'm just content to buy those roses, all wrapped and de-thorned, from a florist. I relish a bracing hike in the outdoors—or at least I relish bracing to be swept up in the tidal wave of humanity surging through intersections against the traffic light. I adore cooking with fresh ingredients, but I am happy to have them magically appear via truck or plane—I feel no compulsion to grow anything on my own (except maybe wiser).

I realize that I may be in the minority. The wide open spaces appeal to many, if not most. I seem to actually prefer proximity to my fellow folks in their infinite variety. Yeah, even that guy on the subway who asks for everyone's attention so that he can describe his battle with city health services—I get a kick out of them all.

So what does God make of this "unnatural" habitat for his children? These canyons of bricks and mortar and glass and steel? These congested streets and jam-packed sidewalks? Is it, in fact, hard to be near God's heart here in the concrete jungle?

At the risk of offending the nature lovers who swear that God gravitates only towards hummingbirds and rainbows and mountain ranges, I offer this: God made us to make cities too. If twin span bridges and high-rise apartments didn't make the list of Creation Day 6, it doesn't mean He doesn't like them. Jerusalem, after all, is a Holy City to three major faiths. New York City, in its way, could be called a Holy City, as could every metropolis from Denver to Dubai. They are all places where large numbers of people live in close quarters. They are used to being jostled together at street corners and wedged into train cars. They are part of a constant crowd. City dwellers have to learn to share a limited space with people of all races and creeds, and most do so quite successfully. The air hums with activity as they fill stores and restaurants and office buildings—and places of worship. The city is a wonderful concentration of humanity, and God has always loved humanity in a very special way.

Some have a hard time seeing elevators as sacred spaces, or hearing the cacophony of traffic as hymnsong. Not me. I can picture the Creator blessing each and every person in the big city, taking as much pleasure in their noise and busyness as in any rolling hills and babbling brooks. And in Times Square—and at 15th and Market in

Philadelphia too—I can feel the raw energy of life itself pulse through the rushing throng of people.
 Pulse just like a Heartbeat.

GREAT EXPECTATIONS

"Reflect upon your present blessings of which every man has many - not on your past misfortunes, of which all men have some."

-- Charles Dickens

Looked at a certain way, my life has been full of disappointments.

I'm not talking about the tragedies, the major letdowns, the deep, deep sorrows.

Though I've had a few of those, too.

No, I'm talking about the petty annoyances and stretches of mind-numbing boredom with which my stint on Earth has been laced—yours, I'll wager, as well.

The long-awaited movie that was stupefyingly bad. *Ishtar*: what was Dustin Hoffman thinking? The bestseller you'd been months on the library waiting list for, then later wished you could get the lost hour of your life spent reading back. *Love Story* comes to mind.

When I was little, days were chock-full of interesting activity. There were Barbies to involve in complex plots featuring pink sports cars and dream houses; there were trikes to ride (never did graduate to a two-wheeler, New Yorker that I was); there were Nancy Drew books to memorize. But sheer boredom was an every night event. I was, even as a kid, a major insomniac. Lights off, the hours crept by at a slower-than-snail's pace. 10 PM, midnight, 2 AM…not a wink. These endless, sleepless nights led to mornings when the dulcet tones of Sister Brendan explaining gerunds to the fifth grade, finally, put me to sleep.

As an adult, I have endured many ridiculous queues at the local Acme supermarket. OK, it's just up the street so I keep going there, but do they really only ever have one register open for a storeful of shoppers? My milk expires before I even get to the checkout. And of course I have sat in mega-traffic jams like everyone else. One night it took me a solid hour to get out of the parking lot after a Billy Joel concert! (And I was so thirsty! And the only thing to drink in the car was warm diet raspberry seltzer!)

These are the times I become acutely aware of my brief span on the planet. Every wasted minute, every throwaway day, really rankles. Why oh why is my precious time being treated so lightly?

I rant. I rail.

But then. I think.

My Uncle Don was born with Down syndrome. His life was not exciting by any measurable standard. Shaving, reading the paper—these were triumphs that took hours. The highlight of his day was watching *To Tell the Truth* on my grandparents' ancient black-and-white TV set. But Don was an inspiration. He concentrated on every morsel of living. Donnie has been gone for almost 20 years, but he is always on my mind and in my heart, especially when I cheer the Special Olympics athletes each November. I am riveted by their beautiful faces, so open and vulnerable and full of life. I am awed by their courage, training to climb steep hills and swim pool laps and lift heavy barbells. Boredom is not in their vocabulary. They take the measure of each second, and find every one fulfilling. And this holds true in all aspects of their lives. They set themselves to a task, and fully commit to it. No bellyaching. No tsk-tsking.

No Great Expectations.

And, as a result, they get it. They truly get it. Every breath is a miracle. Standing before the Grand Canyon. Standing behind the woman with 47 items in the express lane. We none of us earned this giant, beautifully wrapped present called Life. The way we value each priceless moment is entirely up to us.

Can we stop expecting Perfection? Can we even laugh when we encounter our *Waterworld*s and *Jonathan Livingston Seagull*s? Is a gridlocked line of cars on the Schuylkill Expressway really such a catastrophe? Isn't it possible to just chill out and go with the flow? (I can't believe I'm writing this, as chilling and flowing are such alien concepts to me).

Maybe my way of looking at things could use a tune-up. Maybe tomorrow I need to wake up expecting, not Great, but something better.

Tomorrow looks like rain. It could be another Big Nuisance, but then again... I think I'll stand outside, and get thoroughly, wringingly wet, and say, and mean, "Thank you."

MUSIC MUSIC MUSIC

"Music in the soul can be heard by the universe."

--Lao Tzu

It is 5:50 PM on a sultry summer evening in Rehoboth Beach. The traffic turning into the shopping center off Highway One has been at a virtual standstill for ages now, the green light letting, at most, three cars through before changing back to red. Inside my station wagon, the duet *Sympatico* stresses—the violinist and pianist are due onstage in 10 minutes. Finally, a decision: they'll jump from the car and make a run for it. As I watch, my teenaged sons Sheridan (violin) and Evan (piano) sprint across the intersection and race towards their gig at 1776 Club. They make it just in time. For the next three hours, they will entertain the patrons with jazz standards. Afterward, they will return home exhausted—only to head to their instruments and play some more. The paycheck is incidental. The music is all.

It is 3:00 PM on a bleak winter afternoon in Boston. In a studio at the Berklee College of Music, a totally focused young girl mixes sound effects and vocals (some provided by brother PJ) to get precisely what she wants for her pop song, "Tell Me." Whether or not the number will remain in the repertoire as a classic, her 110% effort is given unstintingly. Rose will spend however many hours it takes to make the production of her composition replicate what she hears in her head. Time is incidental. The music is all.

Another Delaware shore summer. The Lewes Chamber Music Festival begins, a series of concerts produced by Sheridan and featuring his stellar Curtis and Juilliard colleagues. They perform everything from a Liszt piano sonata to the Mendelssohn string octet to "Mad Jack's Revenge" (by Sheridan) for brass ensemble. The young musicians stay with us in our rental house, eating midnight pizza and rehashing every moment of every piece played. Sleep is incidental. The music is all.

December in Oreland, PA. *Celebrating Christmas*, a holiday fundraising concert with Sheridan, Evan, Rose and PJ Seyfried, and musical guests, is on the calendar at Christ's Lutheran Church. This has become an annual event for the congregation, and for a mom who thanks her lucky stars that her kids love to play together so much. Each year's proceeds benefit the youth summer mission trips. Precious time, time that is squeezed from brief school breaks, is devoted to preparing for these concerts. Effort is incidental. The music is all.

OK, I get the message. My children are musicians to the core (even Naval officer Evan, who is keyboard-less while on the sub, but still managed to sit in with the band in a Guam jazz club). The music is all. But where did all the music come from?

My warbling, while heartfelt, will never remotely (and I do mean remotely) threaten Celine Dion. Steve has mastered a rousing five numbers on the guitar, ranging narrowly from "Puff the Magic Dragon" to "Charlie and the MTA." The 60's are his decade, darn it, and he's sticking to them! My dad was the kind of church singer people instinctively moved away from when the Hymn of the Day began, lest they risk Guilt by Association. Steve's family had a time-honored Christmas Eve routine of prayers and readings and joyous Yuletide song. One year, sister Ruth's boyfriend Rod celebrated with the clan. As the gang launched into an unbearably screechy "Silent Night," Rod fled to the kitchen, choking back tears of laughter.

We'd have to go waaay back in time to my Nana Cunningham (an accomplished pianist and music teacher) and Steve's Grandpa Clements (a violinist who traveled a circuit, playing music in theatres to accompany silent movies) for any trace of real talent in this department. So you could say that music was a very persistent plant, burrowing up through infertile dirt and a thicket of weeds, unwatered and untended, that beat the odds and bloomed anyway, in the hearts and minds and lungs and fingers of our children.

It is so easy and tempting, as a parent, to take the credit for our offspring's accomplishments. That crazy-good SAT score? Well, Mom DID always do well on tests. That quick wit? Well, Dad DOES make his living as a humor writer and comic actor. It's when the beautiful ability explodes from (seemingly) nowhere that we can clearly see the Giver of All Good Gifts. God created our five and gave them the love of, and talent for, music. Music that blesses them, every day, with joy and with a way to connect with the world. With a purpose—a sacred language, as it were. Hard times in life will come, and go. No matter. The music is all.

So may we each find our music, be it carpentry or physics or football or baking. May we revel in it, and gift the world with it. And then, may we remember, every day, to thank the loving One who is the Source of it. All.

MY BUCKET LIST

"Life is like a coin. You can spend it any way you wish, but you only spend it once."

--Lillian Dickson

They're everywhere these days—bucket lists, that is. A toting up of events and people and places to experience before kicking it. Several in my acquaintance have grand plans and are actually ticking them off, one by one. A friend of Sheridan's was just in Pamplona for the Running of the Bulls. Haven't heard yet if he or the bulls won. All around me people are trekking up Kilimanjaro and working in Nepalese orphanages and eating sketchy local food from Vietnamese street vendors. They are squeezing every drop of delicious juice from life, and God bless them.

I had my list too, back in the day. I was going to (please keep the laughter down to a dull roar) have my private pilot's license by age 18. I was going to tour Europe in an original one-woman show, garnering a scrapbook full of rave reviews. Heck, I was even going to learn to parallel park!

Never even checked off the "parallel park" one.

Well, I'm 54 now. My ambitions have been on a significant diet for years. So I thought it might be interesting to write up another bucket list, to motivate me as I launch into the brave new world of the post-menopausal woman:

1) GET HIGH (endorphine, of course—what did you think?)
   I finally began to run and have hit two miles without stopping. The other day it happened—my legs stopped aching and my breathing eased, right around the one mile mark. I could have run forever!! I called Rosie to brag and

was informed—"Mom, you haven't had that yet? That's the only reason to run!" So...I wanna get high again.

2) SLEEP AROUND

   I am well on my way here. My medication warns "may cause drowsiness"—surely the biggest understatement ever committed to a label. As of 7:30 PM, if you are between me and any surface, baby, watch out! I can doze off at the dining room table, on a chair in the family room "watching" a video, etc. Bed is the goal, but not always achieved. For me, now, slumber is a movable feast.

3) BREAK THE RULES

   My TV favorite *What Not to Wear* is my touchstone here. I will send fashion rules crashing and burning all over the place as I: wear white after Labor Day, wear short(ish) skirts after age 35, keep my hair long for a while. Oh yes, I plan to be quite the Runway Rebel...because otherwise, well—I look at photos of my mom at my age, with her super-dowdy dresses, matronly hairdos and tragic shoes and say—nooooo! Not me! Not yet!

OK let's go for it and throw these in too...

4) BACKPACK AROUND THE WORLD

   Too late? Maybe not. I still own a backpack, so that's a start. I want to experience April in Paris. County Longford, Ireland (my ancestral home) in misty autumn. I want a passport plastered with the names of countries I can't even place, and a treasure trove of memories—a scary night in an Amsterdam hostel, a fabulous Papal audience at the Vatican (never mind that I am now a Lutheran, those Catholics do the pomp and circumstance up right), the Great Wall at dawn. I want to experience it all. Sigh.

5) SING IN A PERFORMANCE OF MAHLER SYMPHONY #2

   with the Berlin Philharmonic. This is the most sublime piece of music ever written, and darn it, I want to be part of it, just once. Note: If this is not possible I will be satisfied by harmonizing with Jack Johnson in concert on "Banana Pancakes."

And on it goes. And I'm sure you have your list too, your fantasies and your maybe-could-happens.

I wonder—what would Jesus' bucket list be? Did He actually get to do all He wanted in 33 short years, only three of which were spent in active ministry? If He had it to do over again, would He have wanted to taste Rocky Road ice cream and camp at Woodstock and take a ride on the space shuttle?

He is God. He could have done it all. And He chose to think local. And small. And to do impossible things in a very mundane and possible setting. Walking from town to town. Giving a healing touch here, a word of wisdom there. It was not the glam life, by any stretch. But it was the life He chose to live.

Which leads me to conclude: bucket lists, even the best of them, have leaks. We can plot and plan all we like, and our future will unfold as it will anyway. Maybe we need to draw deep from the wonderful well of where we are, and pull up a bucket of daily life—the sunrise glimpsed from a front porch, the fireworks enjoyed through the eyes of your four-year-old child, a mug of perfectly brewed coffee. Maybe we should spend less time making to-do lists and more time just living.

Oh, I'm not throwing my bucket list away. I still hope to be the only 90-year-old soprano to solo with the Berlin Philharmonic someday. But if I don't make it...

May I say, and believe, that my life was well lived. My bucket was filled. Exactly as it was meant to be.

ELECTABLE

"In war, you can only be killed once, but in politics, many times."

--Winston Churchill

This is the time of year I truly dread.

End of a long day. Settle down on the sofa. Pick up the remote. Click.

Bill Smith doesn't want you to know his record. A ticket for jaywalking in 1972. $10 in overdue library fines. Bill Smith was once caught eating a grape in the produce section. And he says he's out to clean up Harrisburg! Bill Smith: He should be behind bars, not in office. Smith for Congress? Not on our watch. I'm Jack Scuffington and I endorse this message.

Click.

Mary Jones voted against the spotted loon protection act. She was in the bathroom during the vote on the Grumplesnort initiative. She once approved a hefty 1% pay raise—for herself! Mary Jones. Wrong for Pleasant Acres. Wrong for New Jersey. Wrong for the Tri-state area...

Click.

Tonight on Barry Kling Live. What our nation deserves to know. Where do the candidates stand on Brangelina? On liposuction? On high-fructose corn syrup? We'll find out. Stick around.

Click.

Mary Jones is just plain wrong. Wrong for America. Wrong for Planet Earth. Wrong for the Solar System. Wrong, wrong, wrong.

Click.

Ahhh. Finally. A station without these horrible offensive commercials.

Too bad the show is *SpongeBob Squarepants.*

It's quite easy to be a successful candidate for office these days. You must be old enough to be wise, yet young enough to be cute. You must be very attractive and telegenic, yet still exude a "down home" appeal. To afford a successful campaign, you need great wealth, but you have to live very modestly. You need to be just smart enough, without intimidating anyone. You need a sense of humor, yet never come across as light hearted in these troubled times. You have to have the hide of a rhino to endure the slings and arrows of a brutal campaign, yet still be able to cry sympathetically when appropriate. It helps to have many years of big city experience, and also have lived your whole life in the country. Every human being, from babe in arms to 95-year-old veteran, should instantly be able to identify with you. Any past foibles, flubs or failures are instant disqualifiers.

All that is required is a lifetime of sheer perfection.

You realize, of course, by these standards Abraham Lincoln would be a big dud, candidate-wise. We have become a nation of such feather-light intellectual weight that we prefer to paint our would-be leaders with the broadest of brushes. It's just so much easier than thinking.

But how would Jesus vote, I wonder?

Perfectionism and judgement were the provinces of the Pharisees, no? Those self-important and hypercritical folks would have been right at home in today's political climate I'm sure. With sneers and wrinkled noses they held themselves apart from "humanness" in all its flawed, failed beauty. No one met their impossible standards, except themselves.

I see Him on Election Day, looking deeply into the heart of each candidate for things like humility. True compassion. A genuine desire to serve the poor. Qualities that are often completely marginalized in our contests. I see Him entering the booth, pulling the curtain, and choosing, perhaps, the least likely contender of all. I see Him voting for a real person, not a ridiculous caricature. I see Him electing the sinner who struggles to do better, without pretending to be faultless. The one who dares to wrestle with deep thoughts and dream big dreams, popular opinion be darned. The one who knows what it is like to make mistakes, and who dares to lead anyway.

Perhaps we would do well to be more like Him, and less like the rank-and-file of American culture. Maybe we need to turn off the hate-filled parade of ads and bathe the upcoming election with love. And prayer.

Mary Jones and Bill Smith are not paragons. And guess what? Neither are we. We are all trying our best. Falling down. Getting up again. We are all perfectly imperfect people, on a pilgrimage together. Let's support each other. Let's support those of us with the courage to step forward and tackle the messy issues of the day.

Let's vote on the first Tuesday in November. For human beings that speak to the best in us, whatever the party. That just might be what Jesus would do.

DE COLORES

"De Colores/and so must all love be/of many bright colors/to make my heart cry."

--Traditional Spanish folk song

It's 7 AM on a Sunday in July. The mission trip kids are sleeping, after working as hard as they've ever worked. My friend Liz and I are also on a mission—to get some food for breakfast. We amble, talking comfortably. Even at a leisurely pace, the 7,000-foot altitude makes my breathing labored. We are approaching the open-air market. The scene on the street is literally a riot of colors. The local women wear gorgeous dresses—a rainbow of spectacular hues woven together. Young children, clad in equally lovely traditional clothes, peek shyly at us and wave from doorways. The bright red tuk-tuks (a local mode of transportation, a kind of tiny three-wheeled taxi) trundle along, threading their way through the crowd. Entering the market, again we are confronted by color—glorious yellow pineapples, rich brown wild mushrooms. Guatemala is the most exotic place I've ever been, and I am loving every sight.

    10 AM on Monday. The mission team is hard at work on the site of the future Tecnico Maya School. As we make "cob" from dirt and sand and clay, as we shovel gravel and pour concrete, we see a dream taking shape. Long Way Home, Liz's wonderful organization, is creating a school for the little ones of San Juan Comalapa, using all recycled materials. Absolutely nothing is wasted. Up the hill by the latrine, we sift through bags of trash, and stuff discarded snack wrappers behind chicken wire—these, along with trash-filled bottles, and dirt-filled car tires, will form the core of a wall. The wrappers are slick and wrinkled—a purple bag once held candy, orange contained plantain chips. We stand back from our work and see—multicolors. We raise our eyes and gaze past the worksite. Here we are struck by verdant green—the

neat rows of crops, the trees, the volcanoes beyond. Absolutely stunning, all of it.

5 PM on Wednesday. A sudden storm. Thick tan mud runs down the streets, washing over the white paving stones on the path. Silver torrents baptize us with water. We are much too wet to worry about our sodden shirts and pants. On our soggy walk, we see brightly colored structures in the distance. It is a cemetery, we are told, a joyous place to celebrate spirit and life. Everything about this part of the world is different. The climate, the culture (here, "bilingual" often means speaking Spanish and Kaqchikel). Our senses are sharpened by the newness of it all. And the oldness as well: over the centuries, earthquakes have shaken, but not destroyed, this town.

6 PM on Saturday. The courtyard of the hotel. Oscar Peren, an internationally known painter and a local, proudly displays his work. Oil paintings of people and places, using a palette of brilliant shades—vivid visual love songs to his home. Here, a celebration with fireworks; there, a "chicken bus" (a bus that carries workers—and chickens—up the mountain). Comalapa is known as the Florence of the Americas for its large population of native artists. Later, a trio plays traditional Mayan music on handmade instruments, bright bamboo flutes and tortoise shell drums. It is cold and as we sit to listen we drape ourselves with blankets…stripes of crimson and teal and gold.

2 PM on Tuesday. Our holiday after our week of labor. We are in the colonial capital, Antigua, a magical town of slate cobblestone streets and buildings of sky blue and lemon yellow and salmon pink. Once more, we are bathed in color and beauty.

Our return to reality is abrupt…the sleek and modern Guatemala City airport, flying above the clouds, a stop in Miami, and home in the dark of night. The colors seem duller, somehow. Why is that? Here, people are rushing to catch their flights, are speeding along the expressway. Everything is a blur.

But there, in a remote and remarkable corner of the world, things are clearer. There is much poverty and want, to be sure. There is a landfill where people cart their refuse in a wheelbarrow and dump it into a ravine. Girls are pregnant too soon. Women look old before their time. And yet…

And yet. There is joy. So much joy from so little. There is pride, pride in a way of life that spans centuries. And there is love.

The love of family and friends. The love for 25 strangers, who are greeted with a smiling "Buenos dias" by everyone they meet.

Our Liz lives among them. Liz, who grew up in our church. Liz, who with her husband Adam and friend Mateo, are building a future for a place they cherish. And for the people who cherish them.

We leave Guatemala awash in their joy. Buoyed by their pride. Colored, vividly, by an experience that we will remember for a lifetime.

"De Colores" (Of the Colors) is a famous Spanish folk song, and it rings in my ears today. It reminds me to take out my box of crayons. Make my sky the bluest and my trees the greenest. My love the truest. God gave me the tools, and challenges me, back home, right now, to color my world.

HOLY HORROR

"I have never let my schooling interfere with my education."

--attributed to Mark Twain

For high school students, it's one of the most common dreams. You are racing down the school hallway, sliding into a seat at the last possible second. In a crowd, you still feel alone in the room. The clock is hideously loud, remorselessly ticking the minutes away. Everything you have ever known is rubbed out of your brain in an instant. Basic math. The whole concept of the essay itself. Your mutinous mind awakens, but only to focus on the sharpness of your #2 pencil, the gnat flying into the hair of the boy in front of you. The time passes. Now you intone a silent, rueful farewell to your ambitions, your ivy-covered dreams. Well, so long, Yale. You were a long shot anyway. Adios, Dartmouth. And Penn? What can you say? Maybe you can walk around down there and pretend you were accepted. By hour three, as the whole thing just becomes an exercise in survival, you tick off your "safety" schools as well. In the end, as you put down that #2 pencil and smooth out the answer sheet, puckered with the dampness of your palm sweat, you are resigned to the kind of schools that are advertised on late night TV.

The problem is, for many high schoolers, it's not a dream.

There is a reason that the fall senior SATs occur close to Halloween. They are truly a horror.

What message are we sending our children with this parade of tests, beginning with the confounding PSSAs (the tests that determine the funding a Pennsylvania school district receives)? My children have been grilled like little porterhouse steaks, day after day, to prep for quizzes that mean little to them. Our gung ho elementary school principal started each day with a "PSSA question" over the loudspeaker—piped even into the kindergarten classes, most of whose children are not yet wrestling with right angles. This same fine educator had read that gum chewing somehow increased scores. This was the part my kids adored, coming home with cheeks puffed out like chipmunks, gamely chawing their way through a pack of Juicy Fruit, doing their bit for the cause.

In middle school our offspring are lucky enough to be offered the opportunity to take the high school SATs in...7th grade. This qualifies them for a variety of enrichment summer programs at Johns Hopkins University (each of which costs the equivalent of a major new appliance). Oh, yeah, and they also get the chance to feel truly swamped for the first time. I recall Rose wailing, "Mom, what do they want from me? I've never even heard of most of this stuff!"

Here we are, trying to find a quick and dirty way to evaluate the intelligence of our kids. We get a satisfying list of numbers...1000, 2200, whatever. The kids are badgered into performing, performing, performing. At stake, they are told, is their future in college.

How well do YOU do under this kind of pressure?

Right. Neither do I.

And here's another major problem. Once they've been crammed full o' learning, how much of it sticks? Have we inundated their brains with so much stuff that the important things never get saved in their long-term memory banks? I heard an interview not long ago with an ace test-taker, a recent high school graduate. He confessed that, of everything he studied and parroted back come exam time, he remembers...next to nothing at all. All that work. That 5.0 average. And the kid can't summon up any of it? In terms of actual education, he's pretty much at square one— even as our system rewards him grandly with the trappings of actual scholarship.

How can we stop the madness? Well, we can write to our school boards, our congressmen. We can organize groups of concerned parents. We could all teach our children that there's more to life than written exams. But we can also pray.

Here is my prayer. I pray for serenity for these, our precious children. I pray they look at the beautiful world, and their incredibly special place in it. Of course, I want them to do their best, but for the sheer joy of learning. And when grading time comes, I pray they grade themselves as God grades them: an A for effort, an A for loving, an A for being.

I also pray for an end to these absurd tests. Doesn't life dish up enough worry and pressure for our kids as it is?

Let Halloween and its gentle, meaningless spooking, be the only horror of October.

`Boo.

PLENTY

"Then the Lord said to Moses, I am going to rain bread from heaven for you, and each day the people shall go out and gather enough for that day..."

--Exodus 16:4

"STARFISH!!!" the cry echoed down Rehoboth Beach. We'd been coming to the Delaware shore for at least 10 years, all summer long. The only starfish we'd ever encountered were sold wrapped in cellophane, $2.00/each at the Sea Shell Shop. Yet suddenly here they were, poured in great numbers onto the sand, victims of a rare tide that disgorged them from the deep. Starfish aplenty, starfish galore. Toddlers toddled down to the shoreline with buckets. Those of us slightly older than toddlers also toddled down with our buckets, scooping up this incredible bounty of beautiful sea creatures. How many starfish were too many? None of us was prepared to say. We just kept scooping until our buckets were over-full.

Now what?

Dying/dead starfish...how shall I put this delicately? Stink. So out to the back porch they went. I should mention that the tiny Delaware shore town in which we lived has a rather large population of stray cats. Can you picture the scene?

Yup. Dismembered starfish, munched and crunched by said cats. Everywhere.

We took so much more than we needed (if it can be said that we "needed" starfish at all). The end result? Rot, and loss.

I am a cook possessed. When I encounter a certain ingredient, preferably one that is in short supply, I corner the market. On a mission trip to Costa Rica, I discovered Salsa Lizano, to me the ultimate condiment: a cross between Worcestershire sauce and Tabasco. Then, last year, I discovered lavender, which

McCormick's Spices, happily, bottled and carried in supermarkets. True to form, I bought (no joke) a CASE of Salsa Lizano and an equal amount of culinary lavender. Well, guess what? I actually don't want to use Salsa Lizano at every meal, so the dusty bottles still line my pantry shelf, largely untouched. As for lavender, I probably have enough to perfume baguettes and butter until I'm at least 150.

And I can't forget my wild and crazy spending spree prior to Y2K. Never mind that experiencing the end of the world might actually be preferable to eating a gazillion cans of sliced beets!

The people of Israel hoarded their manna. Maybe God would not provide tomorrow, so they'd better darn tootin' squirrel some food away. You know, just in case. The manna in the desert story in the Bible is huge. The lesson? God will provide, if we just let Him. If we don't second guess, hoard, overstock. Rot and ruin are the end results of not trusting.

There's another lesson to be drawn, too. If we always have too much, how can we enjoy it? Doesn't dinner taste much better when we're at least a little bit hungry? What is more satisfying: one new outfit, saved and planned for, or a bulging closetful, rarely or never worn?

I was recently listening to an interview with the amazing Buddhist monk and peace activist Thich Nhat Hanh. The conversation got around to Heaven, or Nirvana, and the concept of a place of no pain, no suffering, total happiness all the time. A bottomless trough filled with a thousand flavors of ice cream, so to speak. Thay said he would not even want a Heaven with no suffering, that sorrow and joy were two sides of the same coin, one meaningless without the experience of the other. That's a pretty revolutionary thought, but you know what? I think I get it. My love for Steve grew from a very lonely and unsettled time in my life, and was all the more precious for the hole in my heart that it filled. In a poignant way, I understood myself as a mother better after my two miscarriages—and appreciated the miracle of a live, healthy baby much, much more.

If we look at happiness as a passing feeling and not our inalienable right to enjoy nonstop, perhaps sadness will lose some of its power to stun us. Life ebbs and flows—much like the tide that carried in all those starfish that magical, long-ago day. And maybe the afterlife does as well. God provides, today, tomorrow, forever. And He has provided us with the capacity for both laughter and tears for a reason.

So may I—may we—learn to trust God a little more each day, and share our "manna" with each other, as we were meant to do, so that there's enough for everyone. May we treasure the many, many moments of joy God sends our way—and value, too, the heartaches that mean our hearts are growing bigger.

Meanwhile, I'd better work on developing a <u>killer</u> recipe for Lavender, Lizano and Beet Surprise.

TAKING FLIGHT

"I'm not a paranoid deranged millionaire. I'm a billionaire."

--Howard Hughes

Andy Warhol once said that everyone would be famous for 15 minutes.

I'm still waiting.

But there was a moment, a golden, exciting moment, when Steve and I came tantalizingly close to a measure of fame.

And it all has to do with Howard Hughes.

Maybe I should elaborate.

Waaay back in 1994, we were introduced, through a mutual friend, to a very interesting gentleman. A wealthy real estate developer, pilot, and passionate amateur pianist, this fellow had an idea. He envisioned an original musical based on the life of the billionaire recluse Howard Hughes. He'd sketched out a few tunes and was looking for a librettist and lyricist to turn the concept into reality. We were intrigued and challenged. Steve is an excellent playwright, and the two of us had collaborated on many creative projects before. I happen to love writing lyrics. While our subject matter currently skewed more towards the Three Little Pigs than the Spruce Goose (the name of Hughes' legendary plane), we could do this! We were sure of it!

So Steve plunged into research, and became an expert on the life of this brilliant, troubled icon. Though the world recalls him as a tragic figure, an eccentric germaphobe who roamed the globe until his death, Hughes as a young man was more, much more. He was an executive who owned TWA airlines, a pilot who set world records, a Hollywood producer who launched several notable careers. Our show began to take shape. We would focus on the young man of such promise. The play would end at the poignant moment when his decline was assured. It would be a powerful story with humor, pathos, and some memorable tunes. Steve toiled away on the script. We spent countless hours listening to the music, and working on lyrics. The project went through draft after draft. Songs and scenes were added and subtracted at a dizzying pace.

Eventually, *Flight* was poised for takeoff. Query letters, then copies of the script, went off to all corners of the country. We were proud of our work, though trying to be realistic about our chances for a real production. First we heard nothing, then we heard worse than nothing—the parade of rejections began. Long Wharf Theatre in New Haven: thanks but no thanks! Goodman Theatre in Chicago: nix! We started to feel like high school seniors hearing from colleges, as the mailbox filled with the dreaded thin envelopes that said "no way," usually in 50 words or less.

But then, a turning point. *Flight* was chosen as the winner of the Stanley Drama Award for 1999. This is a prestigious competition and was quite an honor, as previous winners included Jonathan Larson's *Rent*—maybe you've heard of it? Scenes from the show were performed at New York's Lamb's Club. It was a gala evening, and maybe the beginning of a star-studded future. Our composer pulled out all the stops—we headed into the Big Apple by limo, no less! And had lunch at the 21 Club! We could get used to this life!

Flight's timing seemed excellent, too. Rumor had it that Leonardo Di Caprio was preparing to star as Howard Hughes in a major movie. Play and film could be a one-two theatrical punch!

The next few years saw some limited flurries of activity—another competition win or two, a performance in North Carolina. We continued to tweak and tweak; this song and dance number in Act One worked, that patter song in Act Two did not. Finally, another possible turning point: *Flight* received two staged readings off-Broadway. A well-regarded director and music director were hired, as was a very strong cast (including 1998's Miss America as Hughes' love interest). We invited friends and family into Manhattan, and both readings went extremely well. Once again we waited for the capital P Production sure to follow such a strong showing.

Since you're not reading this in *Variety*, you can probably guess what happened. *Flight* hasn't made it to cruising altitude. Like most other plays with Broadway aspirations, our show has not yet gotten that full New York production. While we haven't completely set the dream aside, we've come to realize how long the odds truly are. Success along the Great White Way eludes all but the very few.

We've come to believe we're not Broadway superstars right now for a reason, known to God if not to us. While we haven't "made it big," we remain proud of the work we did. Maybe we made it as big as we were supposed to with our *Flight* adventure.

And if we never have our 15 minutes of fame, maybe God has better plans for those 15 minutes after all.

THUMPER

"Thumping: He's frightened, or trying to tell you that there's danger (in his opinion)."

--www.rabbit.org

Lord help me, I've bonded. With a rabbit.

Two months ago, Julie went to a rabbit rescue organization in the area called Luv N' Bunns (I know, I know) and adopted Stoli, a fat and furry white bunny. She had to sign enough papers to rival a house closing—these shelters don't mess around. She arrived home laden with bun plus a small fortune in accoutrements: cage and pen and food and hay and toys. We tried to change his name, as we can only assume he was originally named by a vodka lover. Charlie? Cute, but no cigar. Peter? Come on! Tibbar? My personal favorite, "rabbit" spelled backwards. In the end, Stoli he remained.

We've become pretty comfortable with him. Julie, no surprise, adores him and the feeling is mutual. She can even put him in a bunny trance by laying him on his back in her lap (he totally zones out). Stoli enjoys a certain brand of rabbit kibble, a certain little red wire ball, and, apparently, the Weather Channel. He doesn't shed, doesn't smell, doesn't make a sound and is litter-box trained, thus negating most of my objections. Stoli has, in short order, become a Seyfried, a card-carrying member of the family.

Which is why his bizarre behavior this morning was so upsetting. Out of the blue, he backed himself into a corner and began to thump, lifting his hind legs and slapping them against the ground over and over again. His whole body was incredibly tense; you could see his little heart beating through his fur. My immediate worry was that Stoli was having a seizure, so it was off to the internet and a Google search for "rabbit thumping." What I read was somewhat reassuring—it didn't seem to be fatal, and he would most likely stop in a little while. But why? What was scaring him so? There was a bad thunderstorm early this morning—maybe that was it. Julie had opened the patio door to get his hay—maybe Stoli had seen a squirrel streak across the yard. Whatever it was, something had thoroughly spooked him, and he was the physical embodiment of terror.

It took about an hour for him to calm down. When he did, he relaxed utterly, sprawled on the rug, exhausted and relieved.

There have been many times in my life that I have been a "thumper" too—petrified and paralyzed. Like the time, at age six, I was so afraid of the plot line of my mom's favorite TV soap opera, *The Edge of Night*, that I literally hid in the closet while character Philip Capice tried to escape a ticking time bomb in a building. Young as I was, I still remember my goosebumps, racing pulse, shaking hands, out-of-control panic. I also recall my profound relief when ficticious Phil survived his nightmarish ordeal. Whew! On to the commercial with Madge and her eloquent sales pitch for Palmolive dishwashing liquid!

My fear was about as reasonable as Stoli's, but then, sometimes, fear knows no reason.

Some of my other "thumper" times had more in them of actual peril…the intruder in my folks' Atlanta house when I was 18; the unbalanced neighbor in our Mt. Airy apartment building who threatened to kill us. Along with so many others, I huddled in a corner on 9/11/01, consumed by terror. During the worst year before my bipolar disorder was diagnosed, I was paralyzed very often—how could I get through the week? The day? The next hour?

The scariest thing about existence, of course, is its complete unpredictability. We are blindsided by the frightening moments when we thought all was well. When you think of it, the greatest act of courage is just waking up each morning, ready to face the totally unknown day ahead.

We all have our "thumper" moments, when our wildly beating hearts and rigid bodies have to face the worst of this world. Moments when we are nothing but scared rabbits. Things don't improve by magic. It takes time—and the knowledge that we are not alone—to calm us down, to slow our pulses and relax our muscles.

Can we <u>all</u> stand in solidarity through this terrifying journey called life? Whisper soothing words into each other's ears?

Sometimes all we really need is a little company and a little love to help us keep our demons at bay.

Now, at last, Stoli lets us pet him, stroke his furry back, whisper words of comfort. His heart rate slows and his back legs quiet down. He looks at us, calm once more, and to me he looks grateful. Grateful to us for just being there, for standing with him through his storm within. How could we do less for this cute and vulnerable little guy?

How can we do less for each other?

STILL A FEW BUGS IN THE SYSTEM

"Sometimes I think we're alone. Sometimes I think we're not. In either case the thought is staggering."

--Buckminster Fuller

Warning: the next few paragraphs feature yucky, stinky, scary BUGS. Not adorable ladybugs, not winsome blinking fireflies, not spectacular rainbow-hued butterflies. These insects are the ones you want to hit. Or stand on chairs to get away from. The ones who bite and leave marks, or worse. The ones who haunt dreams (mine, anyway). Bugs: God's Questionable Creations. Read on, if you dare!

In the vast verdant playground that is the Lower East Side of Manhattan (not), my childhood brushes with nature were few and far between. The tiny patch of grass in front of my apartment building was surrounded by a fence and a warm, fuzzy sign: "KEEP OFF." Indeed, when we moved out to the suburbs, it literally took months before I'd venture a toe onto the lawn. I was afraid that police sirens and an arrest warrant were sure to follow. Animals, to me, were either a) securely, if unhappily, caged in the Central Park Zoo or b) pigeons, fat and filthy denizens of the big city, cruising through life on discarded bagel crusts and puddles of Chock Full O' Nuts coffee.

We were lucky enough to live in a building that was not roach- or ant-infested, so I literally never saw Nasty Bug One for nearly my first decade. Then our long series of family moves began. Boy, were things about to change!

Ardsley, New York, 1965. Intro to Daddy Longlegs (thank you, damp basement). Oh my goodness, what planet were those from? I remember frantically throwing shoes at the bizarre spindly specimen, knocking off a leg but still unable to kill Daddy himself. Urrgghhh.

Atlanta, Georgia, 1968. Meet the Palmetto Bug, Cockroach on Steroids, as grotesque a creature to be found—well, just about anywhere. Crunch, crunch, crunch underfoot.

Duxbury, Massachusetts, 1971. Soccer game. Yellowjackets. Oranges for team snack. Note: the correct approach is to <u>drop</u> the orange, <u>not</u> stand and fight. 'Nuff said.

Fast forward through my kids' childhoods. Insect reactions had a wide range: shrieks of terror for some, weird fascination for others. They were munchable for a few, such as Rose in Thailand. A delicacy there is small jumping bugs, swallowed alive—so you can enjoy the sensation of them tumbling down the throat, of course! PJ took things one step further—as a baby he'd ALWAYS crawl straight to the nearest spider web for a snack. Delish! Eight-year-old Sheridan was, for a while, inseparable from his "Bug Box," a collection of plastic and rubber insects conveniently packaged in a small box, complete with its own tiny key. Sheridan later dabbled in real insects, to my chagrin, cultivating a selection of slimy slugs found in the back yard. More seriously, the deer tick that bit Evan in 6th grade at a campout, leading to a year-long battle with Lyme Disease. Less seriously, the beetles of Costa Rica, so gargantuan as to seem almost—benign, pet-like.

I'm no scientist, and I'm certainly no lover of all creatures great and small (humans excepted, for the most part). But honestly, don't most of us tend to look at the vast panoply of creepy-crawlies out there and wonder…what WAS the Divine Point? They seem, for the most part, pretty darned useless. Does God get a perverse kick out of seeing us, totally humiliated, hopping around, screaming and swatting and covered with cute little welts?

I went through a period of reading a bit of science fiction. There was often a pivotal moment in these books when the humans were brought up short by the aliens. We were shown to be slower, stupider, generally inferior. And, always, it was such a shocker. I mean, come on…weren't we "all that"? The crème de la crème of creation? Why were these aliens treating us like, well, like bugs?

Do I think there might be sentient life elsewhere in the universe? Absolutely. As one character in a favorite movie of mine, *Contact*, put it, "If we're the only ones out there, it seems like such a waste of space." So, for the record, here's what I believe…I believe God created everything in the universe. Every jot and tittle.

If there is life on other planets—guess what? The same God made them too. Loves them, too. If there's a pecking order, I'm not sure we're at the very top of the heap, but guess what? I truly do NOT believe it matters. To whom much is given (and let's face it, who's been given more than us?) much is expected. Globally and beyond. God made people (and maybe there's a more elastic, universal concept of "people" possible), and God made bugs. And God loves us all, and expects us to love, and value, each other. Period. Which translates into: why don't we just let the bugs do their thing? Because some days the bug is scuttling across your floor, and some days you're the scuttling bug.

A children's song my kids and I remember with love is called "A Place in the Choir." Here are some of the lyrics:

All God's critters got a place in the choir
Some sing lower
Some sing higher
Some sing out loud on the telephone wire
Others clap their hands, or paws, or anything they've got.

God has His reasons for mosquitoes. And us. We're all in the choir. We all need to trust Him. And let's just try, really hard, NOT to sting or bite each other. Deal?

Bzzzz...

SHADES OF GRAY

"Nothing is perfect. Life is messy. Relationships are complex. Outcomes are uncertain. People are irrational."

--Hugh Mackay

Remember the feature in Reader's Digest called "My Most Unforgettable Character"? These stories usually described people both heroic and saintly. The "characters" oozed inspiration from every pore.

My Most Unforgettable Character never climbed Mt. Everest or cured cancer or was even particularly nice. But she showed me, as no one had done before, how complex people could be. Before her, I thought of my fellow humans in simple, black and white terms—the good guys and the bad guys. Since knowing her, I've learned to see gray everywhere—the basically good guys and the somewhat bad and every nuance in between. Am I glad I knew her? Beyond a doubt. Did I love her? I'm still not sure. For your consideration: My Great-Aunt Rose.

She was born Rose Morris on the Lower East Side of Manhattan at the turn of the 20th century, and lived there all her life. She was the pampered baby of a family that included her big sister Florence (my wonderful, maddeningly self-deprecating Nana) and the middle child, Harold. Harold died long before I was born, but I heard a lot about the hapless child who became the disaster-prone young man. Indeed, until I was about 10, I thought his name was "Poorharold" because that was the only way his sisters referred to him.

Like Florrie and so many other young women of the day, Rose decided to be a school teacher. Unlike Florrie, Rose really didn't care much for children, which made her decades-long stint in PS 20 pretty painful. Over the years, Nana would often learn glad tidings about her former students—this one was a concert pianist, that one won a Pulitzer. Rose would note with amusement that HER past pupils seemed to all find their way onto Death Row. From Aunt Rose I learned the regret of the wrong path taken, but also the gift of laughing through disappointment.

Rose married late, and for money more than love. Uncle Ernest was a rich widower. Aunt Rose had dreamed of a very comfortable lifestyle. Alas, Ernest soon became an invalid, and his care drained their funds and her spirits. The experience made her bitter, and she started obsessively hoarding her every dime. In the end, she left a sizable sum to her only nephew, my Dad (who soon blew it all, but that's another story). From Aunt Rose I learned the poisonous side of money.

Summer afternoons at the Jersey Shore, Aunt Rose would stretch out in a beach chair, ever-present cigarette in hand, and tell stories, some of them pretty far-fetched but always supremely entertaining. Nana would chuckle and urge her to go on. We would sit near them, playing in the sand, feeling the special comfort of children listening to the grownups chat. From Aunt Rose I learned to tell stories well and truthfully—save the occasional embellishment that added spice to the telling.

Rose was a hypochondriac who went on "vacation" every spring—checking into the hospital to have tests run for various phantom aches and pains. She had doctors who specialized in body parts I didn't even know existed. I can still see the cracked maroon teacup that held her rainbow of daily pills. She walked miles every day, and ate such exotic delicacies as grapefruit and yogurt and fish. When Rose died, it was a lingering death from a stroke. From Aunt Rose I learned the difference between maintaining and worshipping the body, and came to understand that all bodies will fail us eventually.

Rose played favorites among us, regularly doting on one as she threatened to cut another out of her will. We all took turns being in her good graces and on the hot seat, a bizarre kind of "fairness." But she never ignored us or acted less than really interested in our lives. From Aunt Rose I learned that we all play favorites sometimes, for better or worse. I also learned never to cut anyone out of my will—not that there was ever anything in my will anyway.

Rose always wanted to be in control, from insisting that Nana leave my abusive grandfather (Nan never did) to walking in front of a taxicab, holding up her hand and declaring "Stop! I'm a retired school teacher of the City of New York. Let me cross!" (she got hit by the cab). From Aunt Rose I learned that there are some situations you just can't fix—and to wait for the green light.

Sometimes, when I look in the mirror, I see traces of Aunt Rose—my dark hair, my hot temper—and I have mixed emotions. But as I write about her now, I realize that I DID love her, warts and all.

And so I paint a portrait of My Most Unforgettable Character, using a palette with every shade of gray. The same gray that colors us all. And I remember that even gray can be beautiful.

SUPPERTIME

"The fantasy is that there exists a small restaurant in the sticks, run by funny, civilized, delightful people, who become your good friends, and almost no one else knows about them. I used to fantasize such people. Now I know them."

--John McPhee

Question. Are you doing what you really love?

Is your job a joy or a burden to you? A calling, or a fallback? What would you do, if you dared to go where your heart calls you?

When Steve and I were on our long children's theatre tour of the Northeast, we had to be pretty darned flexible in the eating department. Pulling into a tiny burg after 7 PM, the only dinner to be had sometimes was a Slim Jim (or the like) at the local convenience store.

So perhaps you can understand our excitement when we stumbled upon the real deal—a very special, largely undiscovered dining place.

One day on the road, I read a long piece in the *New Yorker* magazine, a profile of a mystery chef identified only as "Otto." He emphatically did NOT want notoriety ("Otto" was an alias). His restaurant, according to writer John McPhee, was located farther than five, but less than 100, miles from midtown Manhattan. Other clues were few and far between. In rhapsodic terms McPhee described the place, the site of the best meals the author had ever consumed. Otto was a stickler for quality, traveling almost daily to the Fulton Fish Market in New York City. His wife was pastry chef, conjuring wonders from sugar, chocolate and cream. His small but adoring clientele traveled great distances to partake of this amazing culinary bounty. The article was, to say the least, tantalizing—who was Otto? Where was this heavenly restaurant?

As amateur "foodies," we were keenly interested, and followed the story as it unfolded. Within the week, Mimi Sheraton, then influential food critic of *The New York Times,* had blown Otto's cover. Thanks to her network of sources, she had determined that the exalted eating spot was the Bullhead Restaurant in Shohola, PA (the corner of the Poconos where New York, New Jersey and Pennsylvania meet). "Otto" was a man named Alan Lieb, and his patissière wife was Ronnie. Gleefully, Sheraton unmasked the mystery man and his entourage.

Well, there was only one thing left to do, of course—travel to Shohola and eat there! We feared that publicity-shy Lieb would soon pull up stakes, so we called immediately for a reservation. Spring break was coming up, and, as luck would have it, we were touring schools in Pennsylvania. We invited our dear friend John Carter to join us. John was coming up from Georgia and would meet us at the Bullhead on the appointed night.

We pinched our pennies (this was sure to cost a fortune) and marked off the wait on the calendar.

Finally, the day came. We finished our afternoon performance and drove. And drove. And drove. Darn. Pennsylvania was big. We pulled into the parking lot in the dark. But wait. There was only one car in the driveway. What was going on?

Tentatively, we knocked. A pause. Then the door swung open, and there was our buddy John, wineglass in hand. He greeted us with, "We're the only customers tonight! It's Passover and most of his customers are Jewish! Come on in!"

There followed the most incredible meal of my life. Succulent appetizers were followed by main courses to die for. We ate and drank and celebrated, fully aware of how rare and special this opportunity was. Smoked trout mousse, sweetbreads in mustard sauce, a fabulous paella. By the time dessert (chocolate hazelnut dacquoise) arrived, we were sated. Time for the great reckoning—the cost? We mentally bid our entire vacation stash adieu—this meal was worth the grilled cheese we'd consume for the next month, right?

But then, something amazing happened. Alan, chef extraordinaire, appeared. He sat down at our table with a glass of wine. His wife Ronnie joined us as well. Over the next two hours, we visited with this remarkable couple, learning the path that had taken these two talented Europeans to a remote corner of the Northeast US. Their passion for preparing food was palpable—they truly loved their work, and asked for no "thank you" beyond the appreciation of their patrons. They asked about us, and seemed genuinely interested in John's budding journalism career, and our adventures in theatre.

Midnight. No more delay—check, please! Alan produced the bill. $60. Total. For the three of us. Why? The food rivaled the best of New York, Paris, Rome. But, young as we were, we didn't question. We just paid, with much gratitude.

Over the next few years we returned to the Bullhead several times. We never had a meal that wasn't spectacular—and never got a bill that wasn't phenomenally reasonable. Once we came to town when the restaurant was closed, and the Liebs invited us to their house for dinner (spectacular, as expected).

Eventually, alas, we lost touch. I have no idea where Alan and Ronnie are today. But I find I think of them often, this couple who followed their passion. Wanting no fame, just the chance to do what they loved. Feeding people was their joy, their calling. And if they had three customers or 100, it didn't matter—they put out the same effort.

We all have our passion, our talent, our reason to be. Life is so short. There's no time to waste.

Let's get cooking!

FOUND IN TRANSLATION

"Peace cannot be kept by force; it can only be achieved by understanding."

--Albert Einstein

Do you know how to "hoover"? Can you rap in Swiss-German? Have you ever tried to explain the Amish to someone—in French?

We've learned about all these things without ever leaving our neighborhood.

Steve and I have never been to Europe; however, Europe has come to us. We've opened our home and hearts to a trio of foreign students. Laura, Eva, and Maurus: each in their turn arrived for visits of varying lengths. Each made a lasting impression on our family. Each gave us far more than we gave them. We received the affection of these fine young people, and different, but oh so valuable, life lessons.

Preparing for British Laura's arrival was a piece of cake—same language, right? No sweat! Well, young Miss Greenwood spoke English, all right—but not American English. To her, basketball is "netball"; "public" school is "private" school; you "hoover" (not vacuum) the living room carpet, and you "clean out" the hamster (its cage, I assume, but the Brits don't say). Laura was a delight, and her visit flew by.

So what did Laura leave us with, besides a new way to pronounce "tin foil" (al-yu-min-yum)? The unexpected bonus of Laura's stay was the chance to see our home base through her eyes. She actually found the Philly accent "very interesting." She thought our church was charming (her "local" church is Winchester Cathedral)! She deemed the cheesesteak one of the all-time great culinary masterpieces. Because she observed American culture with keen interest, we took another took. Thanks to Laura, our appreciation for our own particular patch of God's earth deepened.

We discovered that Oreland, believe it or not, might be an exotic and fascinating place.

Eva came to us from Belfort, France the following year. Like Laura, she was a wonderful guest. Here was the difference: Eva spoke barely a word of English. Among the two current French students (Rose and Evan) and one French student from the Mesozoic era (moi), we could cobble together enough French to ask her simple questions, and discuss uncomplicated concepts. But there were complicated concepts that needed explaining too. These included the students' bus trip to Lancaster County to see the Amish ("you see, these people choose to live as people did centuries ago, and…oh, never mind!"). When in doubt, I tended to say "oui" a lot, and hope Eva had not just asked if I'd ever been convicted of a crime.

How did we communicate? With gestures, with smiles, with charades. I often wondered what Eva thought of this big, fast-talking family. She was probably overwhelmed and exhausted by the language barrier, longing to return to the place she literally understood.

On Eva's last day, we were surprised to see her cry. We all were repeatedly hugged and kissed, and then our tears began to flow as well. Eva taught us that we did speak the same language after all. She had come to love our family, and we loved her. So that is what we learned this time around: love is the language the world can already speak…we just need to speak it more often.

With Maurus, we were literally exchanging one child for another, and at the same time. Rose was already in Thailand when he arrived from Switzerland, and he went home before she came back, so they never met. I figured Maurus had little English, and with German student PJ's help I figured out a few phrases to get us through the first days. How American of me to assume! His English, while accented, was fluent. I assumed a lot of other things too—that he was a serious student, with a scientific bent (his father is a doctor), and perhaps a little lacking in humor (the Swiss, to me, made great cheese and watches, but never made me laugh).

So, of course, he was an indifferent student who loved basketball, writing and recording rap music, and joking around. He blended easily into the household, and developed close relationships with each of us.

That year was by far our most difficult and stressful as a family. My mom had just months to live. We missed Rose, even more than we thought possible. My manic depression made me impossible to be around —without warning I became irritated and profane, or impulsive and euphoric. So being a "Seyfried son" had its definite down side. And I felt especially bad because his own parents were divorcing back home in Luzerne at the same time.

Lessons from Maurus? The visitor who casts his lot with yours over time sees your worst, as well as your best. The image of flawlessness can only be maintained so long. Our year with Maurus was a humbling one, for sure. Our family, like families the world over, has troubles. No culture has a lock on perfection. But we are all in this together, and, with enough forgiveness and understanding, we can make it through.

Our small world is getting smaller daily. If we don't reach out to one another, we'll eventually be thrown together anyway. So why not "exchange" intolerance, suspicion and fear for something better? Let's visit. Let's learn from each other. Let's love.

PICKING BATTLES

"Life affords no greater responsibility, no greater privilege, than the raising of the next generation."

--C. Everett Koop, M.D.

When, I ask, will I be approached by Oprah to be one of her panel of experts? I'm ready, willing and able to out-Phil Dr. Phil, at least on the subject I know best: being a mom. Oh, I can picture it now. I'm sitting in that coveted chair next to the Great One. Thanks to the army of hair and makeup stylists, I look like an aging, but still stunning, supermodel. Smiling modestly, I acknowledge the applause of the studio audience, who cheer my motherly wit and wisdom. Or perhaps they are clapping because they're all getting new cars after the show.

Whatever. It's my daydream, OK?

Back to the real world. If you meet me at a party, say, and ask me for parenting tips, you will soon be scanning the room for an exit as I drone on and on. My favorite topics include Potty Training (no matter what you do or don't do, it'll happen eventually), and Punishment: very effective if used judiciously. When Sher was in first grade, he pulled some pickets off a neighbor's fence. His penalty was immediate and lengthy—right to bed (at 4 PM) with no supper. Around 8 o'clock when I checked in on him, he asked plaintively, "Mommy? How long does it take to starve to death?" He and Steve repaired the fence next morning. Those were, as far as I know, Sheridan's last pulled pickets.

At this point, you'll nod and try to sidle off, but wait! Don't go! There's more! How about Curfews? Curfews are a very good idea, even when you have to listen to a parade of lame excuses for arriving home at 11:05—they had car troubles, their cell phone died and they thought it was 10:05, on the way home they had to stop and save people from a burning building, yada yada. Oh, and don't forget about Meals! It doesn't matter what you serve, or what time you serve it. Eat Dinner Together. I guarantee, around that supper table you will find out many Important Things. Where else will you get to hear EVERY detail about the kid who vomited in math class?

As I take a deep breath to continue, and you make a break for it, I will shout after you, "Number One Parenting Tip!! Pick your Battles!!" You will sprint away, but you will sprint away enlightened.

"Picking your Battles" is an apt phrase when discussing the fraught dealings of parents and children. That there will be conflicts, there is no doubt. Your beloved offspring will challenge, push back, defy. They will do whatever they need to do to separate, to grow into their own personalities. And you, the adult, will have to draw the line from time to time. The answer can be, and sometimes should be, "no." But, especially as they enter the teenage years, you need to (frequently) ask yourself: is this behavior/choice of outfit/penchant for thrash metal music that important? How much does it matter, really?

It can be so counterproductive to micromanage teenagers' lives. Instead, I've found, it's wiser to carefully choose what to squelch and what to just let go.

And what have I let go over the years? Things like:

Piercings. They really don't matter that much to me. From Sheridan's middle school-era single pierced ear, to Julie's quadruple-pierced ears, to Rosie's far edgier tongue piercing (gotten, I later learned to my dismay, at the equivalent of K-Mart in Thailand), the odd holes in the skin are just not that big a deal. And they close up eventually.

Hair experiments. Faux-hawks, a rainbow of dyes, chemically straightened, buzz cuts, bowl cuts, 'staches and beards…I've seen 'em all. The kids always think they look fabulous. I often think they'd look better wearing a very large hat and a face mask. But, bottom line, no biggie. And it's all shaved, cut off or grown out after awhile.

Tattoos. As long as it's small and tasteful, I've found I can tolerate a "tat." The only child so adorned right now is—no surprise—envelope-pusher Rose. Her left forearm sports the phrase "check + 48v." Obscure to all but the music geek, it refers to microphones and power sources (I think). More or less permanent, but that will be middle aged Rose's problem someday, not mine.

Daydream aside, I will <u>never</u> be an expert, on Oprah or anywhere else. I can only speak as my kids' parent. Steve and I try to pick our battles, to let the kids make more and more of their own calls as they grow, and to let them own those decisions. Given a choice, we'd rather raise good people than "perfect" ones. And we believe that God cherishes all children, but independent, headstrong, wonderful teenagers in a very special way. Piercings, tats and all.

REBEL WITH A CAUSE

"Good rebels act morally…they choose morality even when morality may result in severe and perhaps fatal penalties."

--Louis Groarke

Dateline: Flourtown, PA. December 21, 2009. 10 AM.

Crime: Parking on the side of the street that is scheduled to be cleaned 12-21-09 at 10 AM.

My first parking ticket. My first ticket of any kind.

Dum de dum dum. (*Dragnet* theme, in case you were wondering).

And so: my premier entry onto the Montgomery County Crime Blotter. When I pull off my big bank job sometime in 2030, you can hearken back to this egregious flouting of Flourtown parking regulations and say, "there were all the signs."

As you may have guessed, I am rather chicken-hearted when it comes to bending, much less breaking, the law. I would love to say it's because I'm so darned morally upright, but that would violate Commandment #8. Honestly? I stay on the side of the angels because otherwise I WILL get caught. Bet the farm on it. So why bother?

Ours are pragmatic lives, for the most part. We do our jobs to pay our bills, we mow our lawns and send our kids to school and register to vote and send in our taxes. We don't complain (at least not publicly). Life just flows so much more smoothly when we maintain the status quo.

But I've been having an amazing, ongoing conversation with Sheridan lately that challenges my notion that God Loves Those Who Go Along to Get Along.

Sher is upset, really upset about the way some of God's people are living. He is upset by the impact of some of his own country's policies on people around the world. He wants to do his part to help.

He's determined, even if it involves personal sacrifice. He's taking a stand.

What to say to a twenty-something with fire in his eyes and passion in his heart?

The easy answer is: Be careful. Let someone else do it. "The poor we have always with us." Change will come, slowly, in time. Don't put yourself on the line.

The hard answer is: go for it, kiddo. Because that's what Jesus would have done, and would have us do.

I am intensely uncomfortable giving this advice, because I know how it flies in the face of my own pattern of existence. Parking on the wrong side of the street (metaphorically speaking) is anathema to me. I don't even eat food one day past its expiration date. I've never yet taken that tag off a pillow ("do not remove under penalty of law").

I was a child in the 60s—as opposed to a child OF the 60s. Anti-war and civil rights protests were the stuff of my dinnertime TV viewing, not of my participation. But I watched Martin Luther King, and so many others who were questioning an unacceptable status quo. I remember the feeling they inspired in me, the passion. I remember wanting to be like them, to live bravely, with such a sense of purpose.

What happened to me? As I aged, I gravitated towards a certain diplomatic neutrality. I came to believe (still do) that everyone had the right to their feelings. But I concluded that, therefore, everyone should always keep those feelings to themselves, no matter what.

But when *is* the time to step up to the plate and register an opinion? Much better yet, take action?

It is, I suppose, clearer when you're young. Wrongs must be righted, plain and simple.

When did I lose that clarity? At what age did I decide that it was better, always, to keep the peace than to speak out?

In Scripture, Jesus had no such misgivings. Wrongs were wrongs, and the time to right them was now. He had absolutely no problem standing up to the current leadership and voicing his protest. He didn't mind the occasional parking ticket, as it were, if it was in the service of a greater good. Not at all.

Timidity has never improved the world. Fear is the enemy.

So how about it? Can we search the corners of our hearts and find the cause or causes that ignite the passion in us—local, global? The answer will differ from person to person, and that's absolutely fine. The idea is to engage the world, and not just let events wash over us.

And then, can we become part of the solution, even if there's a cost?

Do we dare to park on the wrong side of the street once in a while?

As we enter a challenging new decade, what will it be? A blemish-free parking record?

Or something more?

GOING JESUS

"There is hope for the future because God has a sense of humor and we are funny to God."

--Bill Cosby

Warning: some of you will NOT think what I am about to share is funny.

But I am taking the risk of writing this because a) you already know I have a weird sense of humor, b) those of you who DO think it's funny may get a chuckle, and, most importantly c).

What is c)? C is for Christians. And Comedy. And why they should go together much more often than they do.

First, *Going Jesus*. The author of this blog is a woman named Sara, parish secretary of an Episcopal church in the Silicon Valley of California. On her site, www.goingjesus.com, Sara muses, comically, about the fictionalized church she serves (she calls the church "St. Ned of Flanders" in fitting homage to The Simpsons). She also shares a hilariously random assortment of "religious" items that make her laugh. *The Passion of the Tchotchke: Holy Week Kitsch-o-rama* features photos of, and Sara's comments about, super-tacky real items. Examples: *Jesus Saves: The Bank You Can Trust* ("Yes, it's shaped like the Lord in the Garden at Gethsemane...but he's totally happy to hold on to your coins, since it's not like he was busy or anything. Not like it was important. Just bring your pieces of silver over here and drop them between Jesus' hands.") and the *Last Supper Snow Globe* ("Look, I don't care if you ARE the son of God, it's still considered rude to hover over your dinner guests in a giant glitter ball.")

Irreverent? The immediate response would be yes, of course. And yet...Sara seems like a terrific lady, who clearly loves her God and her faith. She's just not sanctimonious. She dares to imagine a Christian worldview filled with amusement, a spirituality leavened by wit.

I confess that I, too, have written religious humor. *The Wittenburg Door* published this piece of mine awhile back (based on an actual event):

"DESSERT STATUE" OF OUR LORD BRAZENLY DISPLAYED IN BIG-CITY ART GALLERY

Chocolate Jesus Creates a Melting Semisweet Puddle of Controversy

New York (where else?), the home of obscene off-Broadway plays, the rap music industry and the $8 cup of coffee, scores another mark on its Wall of Shame. The Lab Gallery in swanky mid-town Manhattan has chosen to display a 6-foot-tall statue of Our Blessed Lord made entirely of milk chocolate. The sacreligous, (though probably delicious) creation is hanging, for all the world to see, during the most sacred week on the Christian calendar.

Sculptor Cosimo Cavallaro has long used food as art. But it's one thing to cover a four-poster bed with 300 pounds of ham, or spray 5 tons of pepper jack cheese on a house. It is quite another to sculpt the Almighty out of a giant chocolate bar!

Reaction to the yummy Messiah has been swift and harsh from the Catholic Church. Said Bill Donohue, head of watchdog group Catholic League, "This is one of the worst assaults on Christian sensibilities ever."

Perhaps the sculpture is a flashpoint for Catholics especially, because they have all given up candy for Lent. At this point, their hunger is intense, and the temptation to break off "just a little bite" might be too much for the growling stomachs of art patrons.

Agitated churchgoers were interviewed exiting the noon Mass at Our Lady of Suburbia. "How can we observe Holy Week now?" mourned one Catholic as he stood, head shaking sadly, on the church steps. "I know it's a solemn time, yet all I can think of now is sweets!" "I'm sick of this crass, commercial and sugary treatment of sacred symbols and traditions," harumphed his wife. "What's next, chocolate Easter bunnies?" Parishioner Jack Doe summarized the prevailing sentiments: "Hatred, disease, violence, war, corruption, man's inhumanity to man: we can all live with that stuff, right? But a Candied Savior—this we have to eliminate! Let's get our priorities straight, people!"

The gallery owners, stunned at the negative reaction to "My Sweet Lord" have canceled plans for a show featuring the Apostles as life-sized cinnamon cookies, St. Anthony as a giant white chocolate truffle, and Pope John Paul II in nougat. They are considering a pre-Good Friday meltdown of the exhibit centerpiece. A reception featuring chocolate-covered strawberries and champagne will mark the festive opening of next month's "Tofu Gandhi."

Jesus wept, for sure…and weeps still, I know, for the pain we continue to cause one another. He weeps for the atrocities committed in His name, by people who use religion as a club with which to beat those who don't agree with them.

But for those of us who cherish humor, who know the power of a smile to defuse tension, who believe it is truly a blessed gift to be able laugh at ourselves….it just makes sense to think of a fun-loving Lord. A God who has created a beautiful and crazy world full of whimsy and delightful surprise. A God who created comedy, and loves to watch us share THAT with one another. Jesus laughs.

So maybe all this won't make tears of mirth stream down your face. But the message—that we don't have to always be so defensive about faith, so deadly serious, so humorless—is a very, very good one.

This year, let's greet Easter, and the hilariously improbable arrival of another spring, with laughter and joy. Let's truly lighten up, and maybe together we can light up the world.

LETTER FROM ELISE

"In the presence of eternity, the mountains are as transient as the clouds."

--Robert Green Ingersoll

Mail call.

Bill, bill, supermarket circular, credit card offer, bill, bill, coupon for Bed, Bath and Beyond. Invitation to dinner—to discuss the many joys of purchasing a spot in a Fabulous 55+ Active Living Community. Menu from Happy Garden Chinese restaurant. Bill.

I'm really feeling the love. Not.

When was the last time I got an actual bona-fide letter, stamped and sent through the post office? It's been ages. "Letter from Elise" is the title of my monthly church newsletter articles, but they aren't actually letters anymore. Until recently, a printed copy of the LINK was mailed to every household in our congregation. Now, everyone with email gets an electronic version instead. Do people print it out to keep? I highly doubt it. Like almost every other communication that appears online, it's probably looked at once and deleted. Much as I would love to think that yellowed pieces of paper decorated with my scribblings will be unearthed by the grandchildren of my audience in 2050, I don't kid myself. Most of my literary output is surely in the "once and done" category of perusal. And that's fine.

What's not so fine, to me, is the demise of the letter—the mushy love letter, the homesick letter from summer camp, the sympathy note and birthday greeting. At one point in my life I saved literally every letter and card I received (and still have them, in the attic). I rarely re-read most of them— there's nothing quite so satisfying as "Merry Christmas 1970 from the Gilmores!" especially when you can't recall who the Gilmores were. I squirm to think of the fevered correspondence between Steve and me when he was in Connecticut in graduate school during our engagement, and have that box on my "to burn" list before my demise.

Some notes, though, are real gifts. After my sister Maureen died, I was, and continue to be, consoled by reading the 30-some-odd letters she sent me in the last years before her accident. I share these documents, written in her huge, loopy handwriting (I've read that the larger your writing, the larger your heart—that was certainly true in her case) with my children and will someday, with my grandchildren, all of whom will never have the privilege of knowing her. The rest of the Cunningham archives may be scattershot. But the Mo letters are the treasure. They would accompany me on a flight from a house fire, no question.

However, I know that Mo would have been among the very first to embrace the new technology. She would have cycled from emailing to Facebook posting to texting and beyond had she been alive more recently. We would have had her funny, affectionate commentary for the instant. But not forever.

Cemeteries have been filling to capacity for years, as our population has burgeoned. More and more, people are opting for cremation—and many of them for scattering in a garden, on a mountain or at sea afterward. The days of the marble headstone memorial are surely numbered. In the overcrowded years to come, legions of people will die and leave no marker, no visible trace of the fact that they were even here. They will only live in memory until, at some point, there's no one left to remember them.

You know what? Maybe it's OK that our written correspondence is, increasingly, fleeting. Maybe it's not that big a deal to have a burial plot that people eventually will stop visiting. Our memories will survive, for a while, in the minds and hearts of those who loved us. But, and most importantly, more than that…

We live on. Our story begins, but does not end, on earth. There's more, so much more, to come. Enough to fill a universe of books. An eternity of inboxes. More content than could ever be captured in ink or on a keyboard. Because of what happened in one tomb, 2000 years ago, millions of tombs are now empty. Our souls will be too busy to jot down notes, too vibrant to rest under headstones.

Everything passes away. Truckloads of letters. Acres of gravestones. Everything.

Everything but God. And us.

SPEECHLESS

"I hate it when people say somebody has a 'speech impediment', even if he does, because it could hurt his feelings. So instead, I call it a 'speech improvement' and I go up to the guy and say, 'Hey, Bob, I like your speech improvement.' I think this makes him feel better."

--Jack Handy

It takes quite a lot to render me speechless.

Granted, even at my most loquacious I am no match for my mom Joanie. She would often, during my childhood, be on the phone with a chum as we left for school. She would still be on the phone WITH THE SAME PERSON when school let out six hours later. Her preferred telephone position: within easy reach of both stove (teakettle) and ashtray (the multitude of cigarettes that fueled her conversations). When ill, we despaired of going to the school nurse for our aches and pains. The nurse would inevitably try to call Mom multiple times, and then complain to us, "Well, your phone line is still busy!" by which point nature would often have taken its course, and our symptoms would be resolved.

But I still would stack my avalanche of vowels and consonants against that of most human speakers. Yakity yak, I chat my way through life, overwhelming all in my path with a cascade of verbiage. In my family, at dinner, for example, if you want a chance to share your day you must take a number, deli style, and wait for a break in my animated recounting of my waking moments.

Now, I actually come from humble beginnings, verbally. As a little girl, I was haunted by a speech impediment. I had a pretty significant lisp, also known as a "sibilant S." If you (unwisely) asked me to tell you who Sold Seashells by the Seashore you would be coated with a fine, salty spray as I attacked the multiple "S" words. Next time, you'd know to ask who Purveyed Many a Bivalve along the Beach instead.

I soldiered on though elementary school, only to find, as middle school approached, that lisps were on the approved list of Acceptable Things to Mock. I spent a lot of time and energy trying to find ways to express my thoughts that had the minimal involvement of the 19th letter. NOT easy, by the way. And so it came to be that I met my 6th grade speech therapist. She was well-trained in her field, and approached my issue with great compassion. While I had my doubts, she voiced none. We could do it! We could conquer this!

That whole year, my therapist mentored me—coaching, encouraging, believing in me. As we worked together each week, gradually my skills and my confidence improved. One day she mentioned her <u>own</u> favorite teacher, a person who had been a real mentor for her, growing up. This teacher had inspired her to follow her dreams—and her dream was helping people communicate. She said, "It's funny—her last name was Cunningham, same as yours." As she went on to further describe this special woman, I suddenly realized that she was talking about my Nana Cunningham, who had been her music teacher at a New York City public school many years earlier. So, the help I needed had really come indirectly from my own grandmother!

I was reminded of all this when Steve and I went to see *The King's Speech.* This terrific film tells the true story of England's King George VI, and his battle with a debilitating stammer. His therapist patiently, but persistently, coaches his Highness towards success. At the climax of the film, the King goes on the radio to simultaneously inform and encourage his subjects about the Nazi threat and England's entrance into World War II. He delivers a clear and wonderful speech, with his devoted advocate by his side.

I think we all need a coach. We all need a mentor—a speech therapist, as it were—to decipher our sometimes garbled message to the world. God hears our every utterance, however we pronounce the words. But God also provides us with partners, friends, interpreters, to help us as we try to narrate our lives for each other. It falls to us to accept that help with grace. And then there's one more thing we must do. We, in turn, are called to the aid of the next sufferer—to mentor, to encourage, to inspire.

We all have a voice, clear or hampered. We need to really listen to, and be there for, each other. That's when the impediments to understanding are lifted. That's when we can all be heard. The song of life is richest, after all, when everyone has a chance to sing.

HOW GLORY GOES

"Science has found that nothing can disappear without a trace. Nature does not know extinction. All it knows is transformation. If God applies the fundamental principle to the most minute and insignificant parts of the universe, doesn't it make sense to assume that He applies it to the masterpiece of His creation -- the human soul? I think it does."

--Dr. Werner Von Braun

Written September 11, 2006:

I'm sitting here listening to one of my very favorite songs, from the musical *Floyd Collins*. The composer is Richard Rodgers' grandson, Adam Guettel. The musical retells the true story of a most unfortunate young man in Kentucky in the year 1925. A Mr. Floyd Collins was exploring Sand Cave, trying to find a route to Mammoth Cave, when his foot became wedged between a rock and the cave wall. During the next several weeks, as a series of fruitless rescue attempts were made, the very first media circus erupted. Reporters jockeyed for position getting interviews and calling in lurid reports to their hometown tabloids, while down below Collins struggled to survive, and to retain some hope.

The most powerful and poignant song in the show is "How Glory Goes." Floyd is nearing death, frightened and saddened by the prospect of leaving the world so early. He wonders what Heaven might be like: *Do we live?/Is it like a little town?/Do we get to look back down at who we love?/Are we above?/Are we everywhere?/Are we anywhere at all?*

I am writing this on Monday, September 11th. Like millions of others, I recall this day five years ago as one when my own thoughts turned to Heaven—what day would be my own last day? And what might await on the other side? I can't even imagine the agony of the thousands of Floyd Collinses trapped in the airplanes, or the World Trade Center towers, as the realization slowly dawned that no rescue was possible.

Every passing has its sorrow—and last moments can often be a time to worry, and to wonder. Is an afterlife true, or not? What comes next? Did I "do" well? Could I have done better with just a little more time? I am sure these will be some of my thoughts.

We none of us know when that last moment will be. But I believe, deep in my heart, we each have a specific reason to be here, and that our time was just exactly the time we needed to fulfill that destiny. And knowing that, really knowing that, means resting in the arms of a God who is always here, there and everywhere. A God who will catch us when we fall. A God who most surely was there to catch the thousands of souls spinning out of the world five years ago today. A God who promises that Heaven waits for us all, and will be far beyond our wildest imaginings. The song ends as Floyd faces his destiny:

> *Only Heaven knows how glory goes/What each of us was meant to be/In the starlight that is what we are/I can see so far.*

We should not be afraid to stand in the starlight when the time comes. In that beautiful moment, we will indeed see. So far.

Written August, 2011: We've made it nearly another five years. This coming September, we will be ten years past 9/11/01. And on the 29th of the month, it will be five years since my mom Joanie died. When she passed on, she was holding the hands of her two girls, and it was my profound privilege to be one of those daughters. I am still light years from having all the answers. But having been there at the sacred moment of death, I do know this: it is NOT a moment to fear. On the contrary. I watched Mom's breaths slow, then cease. I watched as her spirit, her energy, left her body, hovered in the air, and went forward, leaving the now useless shell behind. Freedom is an incredible thing to witness, and I witnessed it that afternoon. I live on, and wait for my starlight moment when I will join her, and Dad, and my sister Mo. Only Heaven may know how glory goes, but I have an inkling. Thank you, God, for the inkling. Looking forward to seeing You.

JOIN ME

"Beware the barrenness of a busy life."

-- Socrates

I took a quick flip through my bulging wallet yesterday (bulging with cards, not cash), and realized I am a member of six supermarket savers clubs. My, that's a lot of saving! By rights, I shouldn't owe supermarkets a dime for my purchases at this point! But seriously, six savers clubs is a little excessive, don't you think? And that's just groceries. I'm also a Barnes and Noble Reader's Advantage member, a member of the Delta Skymiles club (though I haven't actually flown Delta since 1992), and the list goes on. Seems I've been constitutionally incapable of declining when the conversation turns to joining just about anything.

At one time, I was a member of 15 different organizations, ranging from the Naval Academy Parents Association to three different PTAs (elementary, middle, high), two YMCAs (Ambler and Rehoboth Beach, DE), and a Mother/Daughter Book Club. And, almost always, I was a truly terrible member. I would either pay my dues and then miss every meeting, or sign up for a job that I would do dreadfully—such as when, as a volunteer member of the synod Helping Hands Day team, I mailed out directions to the 30 drivers taking youth to various locations. Who knew that you were supposed to affix postage to those envelopes?

You'd think, given the frenzy with which I signed on the dotted line, that my childhood would have been equally jam-packed with group activity. Not so much. Mom was a true "path of least resistance" parent. She would ask, half-heartedly, "You're not interested in being a Brownie, are you?" and look incredibly relieved when I said, "Not really." My sisters and I, therefore, spent an inordinate amount of after-school hours as members of the club "The TV Guides."

Well, I've certainly made up for lost time.

Finally, however, things began to change. When I realized I was speed-reading the month's book club choice in the car parked in front of the host's house EVERY month, I tendered my first resignation. And, to my great surprise, I learned that the world did not end. So I've tried to become a bit more selective in my joining, and a bit more realistic in my commitments. When Sheridan went off to Curtis, for example, it was time to stop volunteering with Philadelphia Youth Orchestra Parents (though the PYO has die-hards whose offspring are now in their forties!) Sometimes enough is actually enough.

I can't really picture Jesus as a big joiner, can you? Filling His days and nights with meetings? Saying "yes" to every invitation that came down the pike?

One of the myriad ways our Lord modeled the perfect life was His sense of balance. He knew when to be with a group, and when to be alone. He always kept focus, and used every moment wisely. Even when the crowds clamored for Him to stick around, to teach one more lesson, heal one more person, He knew when enough was actually enough. He didn't need a bulging wallet filled with membership cards, and, really, neither do we. He knew exactly who He was, and where He belonged. And so should we.

I may still have quite a bit on my plate these days, but at least I'm using a smaller plate. Gradually, I am winnowing some of those clubs from my life, to focus on the ones that truly matter to me. So thanks anyway, eager membership recruiters. "Past my limit" has been a pretty ridiculous place to be all these years. There's a magic two-letter word I'm learning to use, a word that's rocking my world.

The word is "No."

GOLDEN SILENCE

"Be still, and know that I am God."

--Psalm 46:10

Quiet used to be a rare commodity in our house, a middle-of-the night event (unless one of the kids was up sick or nightmarish—then, even 2 AM was noisy). When it happened, that fleeting moment when telephones weren't ringing, appliances weren't humming, and eight people weren't jockeying for supremacy in the Conversation Olympics, it seemed very, very odd.

Nowadays, our household is ever so much more hushed than it was a mere six years ago. No PJ flopped on the sofa channel surfing, Rose blasting music from the band Weezer from her speakers, Evan and Sheridan fighting for control of the piano, my mom puttering around humming "Two Sleepy People." No more of that aural clutter. Nowadays, it's just Steve and Julie and me. Soon Julie will be off to college, and it will be just Steve and me. My husband's daily battle with his misbehaving computer—an education in obscenity for anyone within earshot—will be the only household sound, perhaps for hours.

Will I be able to stand it? Will I become the old lady whose television is always on, *Judge Judy* jacked up to maximum volume?

Or can I learn to love the stillness?

Silence is an acquired taste. I'm so unused to it that after a short while it is hard for me to maintain. I have been trained to avoid awkward social pauses so well that any interval of longer than about five seconds feels awkward. If you are searching for a word to complete your thought, watch out! Here I come, with the very word you are searching for! Or a word I think fits there! Or just a word, any word! Doesn't matter!

My older kids used to do a hilarious and dead-on imitation of me attempting a Godly Play exercise at church, with hand-crafted wooden figures representing Bible characters moving oh-so-slooowwwllly across a landscape of felt. The leader in Godly Play is supposed to frequently intone "I wonder..." and let the words hang in the air, quite content with the lengthy silence that often follows.

Sheridan and Evan portrayed their mother whipping out the felt, hurling little wooden figures into the air and snapping at an imaginary group of stunned children, "It's Jesus! OK? Jesus! And these are the wise men? And what does this mean? Anyone? OK, I'll tell you—they're looking for God. Any questions? Good!"

And I would howl sheepishly in recognition. Loud and frantic, yup. Pretty much sums me up.

I took yoga for a while years ago, and while I could not now do a Downward Dog to save my soul, I still recall my favorite part of the class: the time at the beginning and end, when we just lay there on our mats and breathed. Quiet. Peace and quiet. It was so unusual and amazing.

Can I get that feeling back again, now that all the daily noise is gone?

On those occasions (such as the yoga class) when silence was more or less imposed upon me, I have to admit something magical began to happen. An awareness began to set in, a calm and appreciative consciousness of my body, my mind, my heart. I gazed at a flickering candle; I settled into my most secret thoughts. And in those moments, I could feel the welcome and patient presence of God. A God who had been waiting, waiting for the longest time, for me to just be quiet for a minute. And so the silence became a time to glimpse Heaven. To get a glimmer of what full communion with the universe and my Creator must feel like. It felt strange, yes. But it felt like a gift.

And now**,** thanks to a quiet house**,** I can open that gift every day.

I still yearn for the return of my kids, and the attendant high-decibel levels. I can't wait for them to come clumping upstairs with their heavy suitcases, shouting down to one another, the electric energy of so, so many sounds. The addition, someday, of a grandbaby's laughter will be the sweetest of music. A houseful of noise again will be, for me, a house full of joy.

But in the meantime, may I thank the Lord for this sacred space to meet Him, these surprising and lovely days of golden silence.

Shhhh.

WHAT'S IN A NAME?

"What's in a name? That which we call a rose, by any other name would smell as sweet."

--William Shakespeare

Would the great Judy Garland have been great had she remained Frances Gumm?

Does Norma Jean have the same sexy ring as Marilyn?

And what about the odd collection of symbols identifying the artist formerly known as Prince?

Names are interesting things. Most often we don't get to choose them, but they can define us in a very special way. Expectant parents pore through *From Jennifer to Jason* and wonder...will she/he be a Brittany or a Bill? How does Amelia sound—too old fashioned? Ellsworth—too pompous? Will my current fetus one day be one of the five Siobhans in kindergarten?

My parents named me Elise after a then well-known dancer in the New York City Ballet, Elise McBride. For years I hated the name, and cursed them for giving it to me, all because of a popular ad campaign of the time. It featured a winsome cow named Elsie who produced Borden's milk. Though Elsie was not my name, it was close enough for every little stinker at Epiphany School to "moo" as I walked by.

When the time came to choose a moniker for our firstborn, we were ready. Boy or girl, the child would be Sheridan, a family name from County Longford, Ireland. He is, in fact, a boy, so we added "Alexander" as a middle name. We toyed with calling him Alexander Sheridan Seyfried, but luckily considered his initials and thought better of it. I'll give you a minute. Though we loved the name Sheridan, we were a little fearful that, as a child, he'd be a teasing target. So "Alex" he became for all practical purposes.

Our third, and first girl, had a name fraught with emotional significance: Maureen Rose. Maureen, after my younger sister who died at age 23. Rose, because my sister's favorite saint was St. Therese, also known as the Little Flower. Therese on her deathbed promised she would send down a shower of roses from Heaven. Mo was killed on St. Therese's feast day, October 1st. St. Therese also died at 23. For several years after Mo's passing, different members of our family would find, or be given, roses at the oddest times and in the most unlikely places. There would be a rose in the pew at church, a rose in bloom in the yard next door in the wrong season.

It truly comforted us to hear "Maureen" and "Mo" around the house again.

So of course both kids decided to change their names.

At age 17, "Alex" reclaimed his original first name. He started sending out his musical compositions under what he considered the more "composerly" name of Sheridan Seyfried. We always knew he'd won a competition when someone called on the phone asking for Sheridan. He'd been selected as a Presidential Scholar in the Arts, an honor involving a week of ceremonies and concerts in Florida. He introduced himself to literally hundreds of new people that week as "Sheridan," and upon his arrival home he declared that "Alex Seyfried" was no more. We figured we'd have a very hard time remembering what to call him, after so many years. But our son had the clever solution. If I asked Alex to empty the dishwasher or take out the trash, he would stare blankly at me and do nothing. When I then corrected myself and asked Sheridan instead, the chores were done with lightning speed. "Training" us took less than a week.

Thailand was the catalyst for our daughter's choice. Her year in Chiang Rai as a high school student was so intense and utterly life-changing that she returned to us quite different in many ways. Mo had gone overseas, but when she came home, she came home as Rose. This was a tougher one to deal with because of the sentimentality involved, but we came around, and now can't imagine Rosie being called anything else. And we think her wonderful, impulsive Aunt Maureen would have agreed.

There are as many names for "God" as there are communities of faith. Yahweh. Allah. Christ. Brahman. Lord. Abba. Different as they may sound, each name points in the same direction. We cry out these names in worship, with questions, in anger, in supplication, with thanksgiving. And as I would love Sheridan/Alex and Maureen/Rose equally no matter what they were called, so is our Creator equally lovable, equally approachable, whatever He is called. Our Jewish, our Muslim siblings have unique names for our Almighty Father. And, as much as some think it matters, and thus cause a world of misunderstanding and pain, I truly believe it does not. I feel quite, quite sure that, at the end of the day, He does not care what his beloved children call Him. As long as we do call Him.

    What do you call God?

BABY SISTER

"Having a sister is like having a best friend you can't get rid of. You know whatever you do, they'll still be there."

--Amy Li

Well, I guess she's not technically still a baby. My littlest sister Carolyn (also known as C) turned 50 on May 2, 2011. Wow, 50! Halfway to 100! Poor C! Oh, wait a minute. I am halfway to…108. Never mind.

But to me…she will, always and forever, be my baby sis. As my middle sister Mo and I were only 11 months apart, I have no memory of Maureen's infancy. I keenly remember C's. At 4 ½, I rejoiced at this new addition to the Cunningham family. We had a library of pet names for her. We fussed over her; we adored her. As eldest, I was given some responsibility. When Carolyn wailed, I was to amuse her until her mood brightened. Once she passed the age of fragility—9 months or so—I was allowed to pick her up out of the crib in the morning and change her diaper. I considered this a treat. Mom was no fool.

By and large, these were happy years in our New York City apartment. It wasn't till later that the frequent moves began, and with them the uneasy sense of dislocation. Once we hit the road, we clung to each other as we faced each new situation, and became even closer. I once profiled C in a poem: *Two sparkling green eyes/42 freckles haphazardly placed/Long brown hair brushed in haste/But with more common sense and excellent taste/Than one would surmise* (I was 12. Forgive me.) We bonded on long, hot and humid walks to the Dunwoody, GA swim club for tennis lessons. C endured my cooking adventures in Duxbury, MA with good grace—even though chicken cordon bleu tends to lose some of its luster by its 12th version.

Always, Carolyn exhibited a maturity far beyond her years—certainly far beyond her oldest sister's. When a bout of pneumonia laid her low for weeks, she valiantly completed all her school assignments, even when a fetal pig (we dubbed him "Ethelred the Unready") was sent home for dissection. In contrast, during my three week absence from fifth grade with scarlet fever, I could, at best, have delivered an oral report on the exploits of Marlo Thomas in *That Girl*.

Our lives took decidedly different paths. C attended Ringling School of Art in Florida, emerging as a gifted graphic designer. I attended Georgia State, emerging with my MRS. degree. C's career has been marked by her inimitable sense of style and class: department manager at Neiman Marcus, award-winning realtor, watercolor artist, website creator. Husband Rob came along when she was 30. I jumped into love at 16, and for too many years hitched my creative wagon to Steve's star. C and Rob are happily childless; Steve and I have enough kids to populate an emerging new nation.

After living apart for a long time, we ended up inhabiting the same section of the Northeast, C in Lewes DE and me in Oreland PA. As the locales are only two hours apart, and as we live in Lewes each summer, the new proximity suited us well. Our summer beach walks recalled our Atlanta tennis lesson days; C still endured my culinary flights of fancy—bluefish tacos, anyone?

Several years ago, C and Rob purchased a condo in Hawaii as an investment. We knew they loved Oahu. We just didn't want to think of them actually leaving the mainland for good. But now they're moving away, and I am bereft. Their Delaware house is on the market and packing has begun.

We none of us know when it will be "moving day." While we are still together, let's celebrate our closeness. These family connections are God-given treasures. Big sister, little brother…we are who we are for a reason.

Maybe things weren't so great, growing up. That happens too. But it's NEVER too late to mend fences.

I've often reminded my kids that they will know their sibs longer than anyone else in their lives. Long after we parents are gone, they will remain, with their shared history, good and bad.

Who is in it with you for the long haul? Who lived childhood with you, recalls the same things you recall? Who would you miss, acutely, if they left? Then here's your homework assignment:

tell them. Pick up the phone; send them an email. And when you see them, hug them close. God created us to be in relationships, and no relationships are more meaningful than these. These, the sibling bonds, are sacred.

So happy 50th, C. Thanks for a half-century of loyalty, open-hearted generosity, and unconditional love. I respect you so much, and I'll miss you more than words can say. Keep in touch, baby sister.

DECONSTRUCTING THANKSGIVING

"Let us put our minds together to see what life we can make for our children."

--Sitting Bull

Two experiences I had a few years back have certainly changed the way I think about Thanksgiving.

After my time on the Rosebud Reservation, the story of Indian and Pilgrim sharing a happy feast bothers me. I have a new understanding of how badly, and how quickly, our relationship with our Native brothers went wrong. Any peace and harmony in evidence at that first Thanksgiving sure didn't last long.

Our church youth group arrived at Rosebud, South Dakota filled with excitement and purpose—a caravan of white people in glossy rented minivans. Why wouldn't the Lakota people be thrilled by our presence among them?

Perhaps not so amazingly, they weren't. One of those minivans was quickly scarred with a rock. It took the whole week to even make a dent in their wariness, their reserve. We were the face of those who had systematically abused them, who had robbed them of their spirituality and their culture. The Native Americans had been herded onto the least fertile, rockiest and most destitute patch of land in the state and left to make the best of it. This is a proud people who had once hunted and gathered and shared beautiful stories and created a complex society based on the concept of family (in Lakota, *tiyospaye* means "all my relatives"). Think about it. How would YOU feel if your beloved relatives had been so marginalized, so denigrated? "Happy happy, joy joy" when the descendents of your oppressors came to town? I didn't think so. We tried to serve humbly, to be, instead, the face of those who truly care. Did we succeed? I'm still not sure. But I am sure that it was important to try.

The other experience that changed my views on Thanksgiving? I watched the hilarious but horrifying film about our fast food nation, *Super Size Me*, with our high school youth group. Ever since, I have not looked at a fast food French fry the same way. America is a land of immense wealth and bounty. The downside of that is a virtual epidemic of overeating and physical inactivity: of remote controls, elevators and huge portions. Our kids are the targets of intense food-industry marketing, and their health is in jeopardy. In *Super Size Me*, a group of first graders is shown pictures and asked to identify them. The little guys are fuzzy on George Washington, and totally blank on Jesus Christ, but 100% on Ronald McDonald. It is obvious that we eat too much, and the wrong things. So, at this time of year, tables groaning with stuffing and pie do not hold much appeal.

It would be easy to feel uneasy, queasy and guilty as the fourth Thursday in November approaches.

But wait. When I deconstruct Thanksgiving, unpack old notions and habits, can the day still be an occasion for grace and gratitude, instead of gluttony and guilt?

We are a truly great country, but we rewrite our own story at our souls' peril. We can still be proud of America when we look honestly at America's mistakes. It takes great courage and decency to own these mistakes, and to do what we can to make things better from here on out. We can extend helping hands and loving hearts to people who have been wronged. And so, little by little, things get better. Healing happens. Reflecting honestly on the past can lead to a much brighter tomorrow.

We are incredibly lucky to have the food choices we do. We have the power to select only the best, freshest and most wholesome food to enjoy together around our holiday table. We can get out of the drive-thru lane and relax with our loved ones, share warm feelings and conversation along with the mashed potatoes. We can take a long walk together after the dishes are done, and enjoy the beauty of God's creation in the company of our favorite people. This can be a grace-filled meal, and an experience we can repeat often by eating together intentionally, grateful to have another day to share.

May this be a time of candor about our past, balance in our present, and hope for our future. I invite you to take a different look at Thanksgiving this year. And I wish you and your families a wonderful day.

GONE FISHIN'

"There are many kinds of success in life worth having…but for unflagging interest and enjoyment, a household of children, if things go reasonably well, certainly makes all other forms of success and achievement lose their importance by comparison."

--Theodore Roosevelt

For good or ill, my children know me well. They know how very much I love them, but that I do not love them enough to go fishing with them. I would walk over hot coals for them, but I will not take them out to practice driving on the expressway. I will stay up till the wee hours with them to soothe a fevered brow, but a sunrise bike ride to the state park? Sorry, but no dice!

As a newlywed, my hope chest, as it were, contained volumes of cookbooks and lots of records (the LP kind) and rather too many clothes. If we were planning to open a high-end restaurant with spiffy background music and nightly fashion shows, I was armed and ready. Steve, on the other hand, brought to our sacred union an array of power tools and fix-it gadgets, a library of play scripts, and the hot pink shirt/plaid pants combo he'd been sporting since his groovy college days. Again, we were in tip-top shape if the need arose to build a stage for a production of *Waiting for Godot* set in 1968 Valdosta, GA. Together, we figured, we had life pretty well covered.

Once the parade of children arrived, I would happily re-read *The Runaway Bunny* until I was, literally, the Bunny Whisperer. Steve soon wearied of The Endless Storytime. However, he relished bouts of spirited roughhousing, with me in the background fretting, "Don't turn him upside down!! Don't swing her around like that!! Be careful, for God's sake!!"—my warnings barely audible under the yelps and crows of childish delight. I was Beach Mom. He was

Nature Hike Dad. Together, we figured, we had this parenting thing pretty well covered.

Growing up, however, my folks had another take on all of this. They often operated as if they were still childless, indulging their proclivities without considering if they might in any way pertain to us. In Tom and Joanie Land, the kids fit (or did not fit) into the parents' interests. If the answer was "did not fit," well then, too bad for us! Mom's ideal day included 20 (yes) cups of tea, an equal number of cigarettes, and an intense talk-a-thon (didn't matter with whom). We three girls were so starved for her attention that we learned to sit, caffeine and nicotine-less, and pretend to love love love chatting. Dad was even more rigid. On the rare occasions that Mom left us for the day to visit her own parents in suburban Larchmont, Padre planned his afternoon precisely as if we did not exist. We would (oh, joy) wash his station wagon for him under the viaduct, ride out to watch the planes take off at Idlewild Airport (a passion of his, not ours), and finish the fabulous fun with Dad and Grandpa (Pop), perched on barstools in a beery-smelling, dimly lit bar and grill, swilling our Shirley Temples while the men imbibed somewhat stronger beverages.

These days, I am negotiating the uncharted waters of parenting twenty-somethings. These alien creatures text and email me irregularly, call me at the crazy hour that suits them—most often during my nightly coma. They live in far-off cities and work at little-understood jobs.

When they are home, they gamely fall back into the Seyfried Offspring Pattern, enjoying Mom's home cooking, hiking and biking with Dad. But there is a gulf-sized gap between me and my children now, and I feel it keenly. Evan waxes eloquent about the submarine's nuclear reactor. Rose is now a "Foley artist." Sheridan attempts to school me on counterpoint, and PJ patiently goes over the subtleties of lacrosse refereeing. Julie is still a teen at home; her daily burden is bringing me up to speed on pop culture in general. I try hard, but it all passes through my cranium in a blur…circle of fifths…steam turbine…moves and specifics…scorecards…Lady Gaga…

Sometimes I feel like I'll never catch up. I will be the ancient crone (like Steve's great-grandmother) who shouts "Be quiet, you devil!" at the ringing telephone. I will forever cheer the wrong team, and nod blankly at Evan, and smile vacantly at Sheridan. I will miss the mechanics of Foley, and the point of *Pretty Little Liars.*

As my brain explodes with all the new data, I wonder: what is the better path? To hold my ground and just do what I love? Or to reach over the chasm, and attempt to understand what my kids are passionate about? Friends of mine, fellow parents, are in both camps. I know I certainly don't want to BE my children's contemporary—I've seen folks try it and it's not a pretty picture. But at the end of the day, will the young Seyfrieds prefer to remember Mom and Dad clinging to their Fave Activities? Or will we get some props for encountering THEIR world, a world without pink polyester shirts and scratched-up LPs and Shirley Temples in a New York tavern?

I tend not to trust my instincts. They have led me into the briar patch too often. But this time, I'm getting a pretty clear message that I might do well to heed.

I need to keep trying. Not abandon my old loves (the kids may well come to love them, too), but step out of my comfort zone. Bait a hook and go fishin' with them once in a while, and just see what I can catch.

HALFWAY HOME

"Is death the last sleep? No, it is the last final awakening."

--Walter Scott

The worst thing I could imagine, had happened. Maureen, my beautiful, funny, headstrong sister, was dead. Mo had lived her life at 200 mph, taking too many chances, most in the name of love—love for her family, love for her friends. So perhaps it was no great surprise that she met her fate in a car. In one horrific moment, crumpled against a utility pole, Maureen's short time on earth came to a violent end.

Steve and I were living in Philadelphia when she died in Atlanta. To my last day I will recall exactly where I was, standing in my living room when my sister C called the first time—there'd been an accident; she was on her way to the hospital. And the second call, an hour later: "Can you come home today, please?" Numbly we went through the motions. Dealing with the wreck of her Mazda. Choosing a casket, the last thing anyone should be choosing for a 23-year-old. Everyone began to gather for the wake and the funeral. My New York family sent representatives down—my two uncles, mom's brothers Jack and Gerry. But my Grandma Berrigan (Mom's mom) was not with them. And there was a reason for that.

Grandma was battling Alzheimer's disease. We decided not to frighten and confuse her with this tragic news. There was no point—what could she do about it? Besides, she would not be able to retain the information anyway, and the idea of repeating it over and over was unbearable. But we were especially saddened, because Grandma had always had a soft spot in her heart for Mo, the middle child. Mo had really loved her visits in the Larchmont kitchen, tea and cookies and lots of laughter. Grandma would never, *should* never know of Maureen's death, and that was hard to think about.

Life went on. After several months, my mom was finally able to travel north and visit Grandma. Mom approached the house, her heart sinking. She anticipated a familiar litany of questions. Grandma always asked about the granddaughters in order. What would she say when it was Maureen's turn? And so it began today. "How is Elise?" "She's married, to Steve, Mom. They live in Philadelphia." But, instead of asking for Mo, Grandma skipped ahead, "And dear little Carolyn?" "She is doing well, still living in Atlanta."

There was a pause. "And the little one who died."

What? No one had told her. Mom was sure of it.

Calmly, Grandma continued. "Maureen. Yes. She comes to me, you know. Sometimes at night, sometimes when I'm sitting in my chair.

"When I see her, it looks like she's walking along beside a fence, and I am on the other side. She talks to me. Lovey, Maureen didn't want to go out that night. She wanted to stay home. Her friends called after you were asleep."

My Lord, thought Mom. She remembered finding Mo's scrawled note to the same effect on the kitchen table. She found it in the early dawn, after the police knocked on the door. *That's right. But how could she…?*

"Dear, Maureen needs you to stop crying. She is fine. She's very happy, except that she's worried about all of you. Your tears are holding her back from where she needs to go next."

Mom's tears flowed freely, right now. For this miracle.

The incredible visit continued. Grandma was more alert than she had been in several years, not repeating a single question. When it was time to go, she took Mom's hands in both of hers and squeezed. "Maureen loves you so much. Please let her go."

Grandma lived another 12 years. She and Mom never had another lucid conversation. She never mentioned Maureen again, to anyone.

Back in Atlanta, Mom shared the amazing story with a priest who was a close friend of the family. Father Lopez offered this: *People with dementia live with one foot on earth, and one foot in Heaven.* Grandma was halfway home. Anything can happen when you're halfway home to God.

It has been 27 years. They're all home now, all the way home: my sister Maureen, my Grandma, my mother. And the rest of our family waits to join them, with longing, with thanks. And with the most blessed assurance.

BUSY BEE

"Fame is rot; daughters are the thing."

--J.M. Barrie

Let me put it right out there: Julie Claire Seyfried is the kind of girl I always loved to hate. Julie has long blonde hair that looks good in any style. I had frizzy brown hair, and any efforts to straighten it (with the big household iron) or lighten it (with lemon juice) were doomed to failure. Julie also has lovely unspotted skin. When my friend Lisa Axelberg coated my face with horseradish, as per her mom's home remedies book, I burned off several layers of epidermis, but found that every last one of my hideous freckles remained behind. Julie's slender figure is the natural result of plenty of regular exercise and the right foods. As a teen, my slender figure was painfully attained by such means as Dr. Stillman's Quick Weight Loss Diet (just one hamburger patty and 3 hardboiled eggs per day, providing all the hunger headaches your body can produce), and short-term exercise frenzies (playing tennis in 90 degree Georgia heat until I fainted from the exertion).

Jules is as comfortable with males as she is with females, and counts many boys as friends. My youthful feelings for the opposite sex ranged from terrified (whenever they looked in my direction), to repulsed, when they did those goofy guy things—like the time John Albert ate a box of Crayola crayons in first grade to impress me. He threw up in 8 Brilliant Colors. Julie has very independent taste in movies and tunes. She loves 1930's screwball comedies and 1940's big band sounds, and doesn't care a bit if the "in" crowd disagrees. I used to carefully hide my love for Dickens novels and Beethoven symphonies when the popular verdicts on them were "boring" and "stupid."

And, darn it, she's nice to boot. So even back in the day, I don't think I could have hated Julie after all.

As the caboose of the long Seyfried train, Julie got the last random bits of my patience and attention. She was often dropped off for the game and picked up when it ended, after I had hit my lifetime limit of soccer spectating. She was woken from her nap so I could go get a sick brother or sister at school. In later years, Julie sick at school waited for her pickup, fever spiking, as I finished up just one more thing at work first. Her clothes were hand-me-downs (some of them handed down four previous times), and her board books came to her pre-chewed by previous teething siblings. Baby Sheridan dined like a little king on homemade applesauce and pureed fresh carrots. By the time Julie rolled around, her dinner was the family dinner, take it or leave it (which is why she so early came to love things like four-alarm chili and mu shu pork—it was consume or perish). And, worst of all, she's been left behind as, one by one, her beloved Big Kids have gone off to college.

Given the choice of being resentful or resourceful, Julie has chosen the latter. She's game to try, and to learn, anything. Long ago, we used to call her Worker Bee, so busy and happy a toddler was she, especially when drawing pictures. I'll never forget the time we came home to find Jules in frustrated tears, and our perplexed babysitter Beth, who told us, "She keeps saying 'Wahkabee, Wahkabee' and I can't figure out what she wants!" As soon as the paper and markers appeared, all was well with Worker Bee once more.

Nowadays she is still our Busy Bee. She hustles to make her own money, currently holding four jobs (sitter, house cleaner, waitress in a retirement community dining room, box office helper for our theatre), and she runs cross country in high school as well. She's starting, à la Rose, to travel on her own (London last summer), and participates in all the church mission trips. She's thinking of a career as a geriatric nurse. The gentle and loving way she helped out during my mom's last years leads me to think she'll be a fine one.

Not to say she's always sweetness and light. Bees, after all, can sting. She can talk back to beat the band when she's in a mood. She can stomp to her room with the pros. She and PJ, like Rosie and Evan before them, have had more than a few rather heated "disagreements." Her canonization as Saint Julie is probably a few years off yet.

But I'm always amazed at the person she has become, short-changed and neglected as she sometimes was. She reminds me that

Someone else had a hand in raising her, who taught her how to love so, so much—even when her overwhelmed parents fell short.

So what will we do when our bee buzzes away at last?

I know what I will do. I will cherish every memory of my Fifth and Final, our happy surprise. When I'm lonely for her, as I surely will often be, I will do what she loves to do: I will straighten up the house, light some candles and play soothing music. Julie can make a house a home like no other, and I know she'll do that wherever she goes.

And wherever she goes, she will always be the piece that makes the Seyfried puzzle complete. The piece with all the beautiful colors. The piece that connects the rest of us together. The one we've needed all our lives.

A NOVEL IDEA

"There are many reasons why novelists write – but they all have one thing in common: a need to create an alternative world."

--John Fowles

Not a surprising announcement, this: I love to write. Poetry, essays, plays. It is more than a satisfying form of creative expression for me. Writing has saved my life on more than one occasion. When I am so happy, or so sad, that I can't even speak, I can always write.

So it IS perhaps a surprise that I never gave writing a novel a shot before. But it always seemed to be the most complex, intimidating, and, yes, tedious project of all: creating a boatload of characters, dreaming up a compelling, yet coherent, plot that would take the reader on a fascinating journey. Disciplining oneself to write many hours per day, squeezing writing in between business meetings and changing diapers. How discouraging, not inspiring, to read that John Grisham penned his first few novels at dawn, writing on legal pads, before leaving for his practice; that the über-prolific Danielle Steel tossed off her tomes while raising nine children. They seemed to me quite superhuman. If this was a novelist, then a novelist was not me. Back to my jazzy little poems, as short as I wanted them to be!

Late last month, a good friend of mine mentioned that November was National Novel Writing Month (come on, you knew that already, right?) He, and several other friends of his, were going to take the following challenge: on the NaNoWriMo (yes) website, they would join thousands of others who would try to write an entire novel (175 pages, 50,000 words) between November 1st and 30th. I checked out the website, and it just sounded like too much fun to resist. An international community of people, racing to deadline. No cash prizes or big publishing contracts involved. Just the chance to jump off the high dive and see if you can do it.

Anyway, I'm having a total blast. I have made no intricate schematics of plot and character. I just boot up the computer and write. I started out using three main characters only, everyone else was a walk-on. I wrote my first sentence without a clue in the world about who these people would be, and what would come next. As I typed, and the hours flew by, the words just appeared. By the end of my first session (Lord, look at the time. Has it really been four hours?) I had discovered that I actually had six characters sharing the same three names. In every odd numbered chapter the characters appeared darkly comic. In the even chapters, they were tender and sweet. And the chapters kept flipping back and forth until the characters started invading each other's chapters. So eventually it seemed like there were just three characters after all.

Oh, I know it sounds complicated, but trust me, it's working without much effort on my part.

I'm at almost 20,000 words, and it's only Nov. 8th as I write this. My novel is my treat to myself when the dishes are done, work is over for the day, and the kids are settled.

I really don't care if what emerges at midnight Nov. 30th has a future as a book. I would truly be shocked if it appeared on the front table at Barnes and Noble. Trust me. Truly shocked. What matters is, I conquered the fear, the fear that I would never be able to do this.

The director of the project, Chris Baty, writes:

Novels are not written by novelists. Novels are written by everyday people who give themselves permission to write novels. Whatever your writing experience, you have a book in you that only you can write. And November is a beautiful month to get it written.

I will expand on that even a bit more.

We are the authors of our lives. Our lives are our novels. We can be as creative as we want, and it's all right. It's our "book," no one else's. Some of us prepare painstakingly, some "wing it." There is a final deadline for our "project" (not as clear as for the novel itself of course). Tough things will happen beyond our control, and our job as authors is to take these events and shape them into something better in the next chapter. Something beautiful.

We have God-given passion and promise that makes it possible, more than possible, to make our lives works of art.

How can we ever be thankful enough to Him for that? The freedom to be our unique selves, making our own choices in every chapter—that's the way He planned it. We aren't helpless puppets. We are His most beloved children. Just as we delight in the independence and creativity of our own children, so He delights in us.

So, write your novel, as I write mine. The amazing, incredible, tragic, funny and lovely story of you. And good luck to all of us.

BLESSED BE THE TIES THAT BIND

"Then Peter began to speak to them: 'I truly understand that God shows no partiality, but in every nation anyone who fears Him and does what it right is acceptable to Him.'"

--Acts 10:34-35

In my office at church, there is a beautiful icon of Saints Peter and Paul, a gift from Eastern Orthodox friends. When I gaze at it, I can smell incense. I can hear prayers in Greek, in Russian, in Albanian. I can see babies lifted in their parents' arms to receive the Eucharist (bread bits soaked in wine), on a tiny spoon. I remember the Orthodox priest, so warm and welcoming that he invited one of our own young people to put on a gold robe and serve as one of the acolytes.

On any given weekend, all over the Philadelphia area, people of all backgrounds, all ages, all colors, gather for worship. They gather in temples, in mosques, in synagogues, in cathedrals and chapels. Ever wonder what it would be like to join them? To meditate with a Buddhist priest? To discuss prayer with a Muslim leader? To soak up the blissful quiet of a Quaker meeting? For the past nine years, our Confirmation classes have been able to do just that. Moreover, they have helped raise the roof in glorious song with a 100-member Baptist gospel choir; they've enjoyed a delicious Friday night supper and Shabbat service with our Jewish neighbors at a nearby synagogue; they've attended Hindu worship at a temple filled with golden statues, flowers and food, music and dance.

Everywhere we have traveled, we have learned so much, and been greeted with such kindness. Mennonites, Unitarians, Baha'i…all have gone out of their way to share their faith stories, and to make us feel welcomed in their midst. Everywhere we have traveled, we have been struck by the differences in the various faiths, certainly, and the elements of the worship services. There are readings from the Bible or the Torah, the Koran or the great philosophers. Music ranges from rhythmic chants to traditional hymns to haunting Hebrew melodies. When there is Communion, it can be Wonder bread and water, instead of pita bread and wine.

Everywhere we have traveled, though, we have also been delighted by similarities—the ties that bind us together as people of faith. We share a belief in a Creator, we share a call to show love in the world, with generosity, honesty and compassion. We have a reverence for the sacred, and feel a call to honor the sacred in every heart. We all sense that people of faith touch a deeper reality than the surface of everyday existence—a reality that gives life its meaning.

When I first came to Christ's Lutheran Church, one of my first tasks was making some changes in our Confirmation program. An idea that appealed very strongly to me was giving the students the chance to learn about MANY other faiths, Christian and non-Christian alike. I came from the Catholic Church of the early 1960s, where exploring other religions was definitely not encouraged. I grew up on stories like my mom's ill-fated romance with a fellow named Frank Schaffer. Their love was doomed, largely because of his "very different" faith tradition: he was (gasp) Episcopalian! But as I've aged, I have expanded my view on the subject widely. I believe that wondering about our fellow travelers' different spiritual paths and practices is normal, and healthy. Moreover, understanding leads to friendship, and friendship in our global village is the only way we will ever finally stop demonizing and destroying one another. Finally, I have confidence that my Lutheran faith stands up to honest questions, to scrutiny, to comparison; I'm not afraid for the kids to learn about other religions. I truly believe students who have learned about other faith communities firsthand will have a deeper understanding of the creed they choose to affirm on Confirmation Day.

God loves us <u>all</u>. Let's revel in that love, and celebrate the ties that bind us together, and together pray for a beautiful, peace-filled world where we all can live as His children.

STRANGER IN PARADISE

Waikîkî i ke kai mâlamalama   Waikiki in the glimmering sea
He wai ho`oheno a ka pu`uwai   Cherished waters of my heart

                 -- O`ahu (Traditional)

Aloha!

It's a glorious, sunny morning on Evan's lanai (porch) in Honolulu. I am simultaneously balancing a laptop and a mug of Kona coffee, gazing out at the magnificent ocean view, and pinching myself (picture that if you will). I cannot believe I am here. The whole time Evan's been stationed at Pearl Harbor I figured there was no way I'd ever be able to visit him. Then Rosie picked up stakes and moved to Seattle in February, so there were two kids I could no longer see.

Suddenly, miraculously, everything changed. I found myself booking an itinerary that would take me to both Ev and Rose in the same trip. I was going to Oahu, with an overnight layover, both ways, in Seattle!

The manic preparations began. I packed enough for a seven month stay, which was great except that I was only staying seven days. So I unpacked 2/3 of it and was ready to go. True to form, I left oodles of instructions for everyone while I was gone. Would anyone at church remember to set out crayons, as well as paper, for the Easter breakfast craft table? Better make a note of that! Would Julie remember to feed her fish, as she has without prompting for the last year and a half? Better remind her five or six times! The madness continued as we pulled out of the driveway en route to Philadelphia International, me still calling out directives (Trash pickup Friday! Unplug the iron after use!) until the family chorused, en masse, "Will you please shut up?" That darned family! See, they miss me already!

So began the longest solo trek I have ever made. No travel companion at the airport, in the sky, in the hotel room. No one to share the exasperation of rain delays and a missed connection. No one to toast when the flight attendant passed out the complimentary mai tais over the Pacific. I read a book, and couldn't concentrate. I longed to sleep, and couldn't doze off. Try as I might, I couldn't shut off the boring, droning voice inside my head. Who had invited ME along, anyway? What a drag! After 54 years of busy-ness and more or less constant company, I came face to face with a cold, hard fact: I'd rather be with somebody, ANYbody, than be alone.

After a brief but great visit with Rosie, I proceeded to Hawaii. The first hours were wonderfully full of treats and distractions. Evan greeted me with a beautiful orchid lei; we took an evening stroll at Waikiki and had a long catch-up talk over dinner. With relief, I plunged back into the world of other people.

But Evan is on duty today, and I am once again on my own. This will be the pattern for most of the days I am here. Amazingly, a visit from his Mommy did not much impress the US Navy. If I drive him to Pearl I can have the car and explore the island during the hours he's at work.

So where should I go? To Kailua Beach? Hike Diamond Head? Find a local farmer's market? Do I even know what I want? Have I ever before shut off my auto-pilot, paused in my dance of actions and reactions with others to find out? It's so scary—I'd much rather join a horde of camera-wielding Japanese tourists on a bus to <u>anywhere</u> than set off to somewhere with only Elise. Elise, who dogs my footsteps like an annoying identical twin. She who talks too much and reflects too little. Elise who, left to her own devices, hasn't got the first clue what to do. It seems that what I'd really love is a vacation from me—and I can't have one.

So here I sit on the lanai, a stranger (to myself) in Paradise. It won't be easy to change the habits of a lifetime, but I realize I just can't afford to waste these few golden days. I take another sip of coffee, and a deep breath, and make a choice. I will head on out, somewhere, alone. Since I can't shed myself like a snakeskin, I will use this time to get acquainted with the inhabitant of my body, and to make my peace with her. Soon I'll be home again, with the million sounds of my jam-packed life to drown out my own voice once more. Until that happens, though, I pray I can listen to that unique voice without automatic dislike. Find a way to actually relish being solitary.

May this be the week I finally learn to tolerate, and perhaps even enjoy being with, the person I am. And who knows? I just may leave Honolulu with a brand new friend. Me.

IF THE SHOE FITS

"If you are not doing what you love, you are wasting your time."

--Billy Joel

Hey, folks, just finished another week of altar guild duty! This was my third (I think) turn, and the first time I operated without close supervision. So, just so you know: yes, I am the person who crammed the lovely flowers helter-skelter into the holder to be delivered to a congregational member unable to worship with us. I'm sorry. I also managed to: turn a pair of white gloves filthy with green and brown residue from said flowers, hastily rinse and poorly dry the vases, leave the offending gloves wrapped in a tea towel in my pew (I was going to take them home to wash) and, as a piece de resistance, I left the sacristy door open. Whoever saw the gloves and towel and took them to clean, thank you. Whoever shut the sacristy door, thank you. Fair warning: I'm on the schedule again soon. For Communion Sunday. It won't be pretty.

For whatever my well-intentioned reason, I signed up (and signed my Julie up) for altar guild. I knew they needed extra help, and, frankly, the incredible people who serve in this ministry do so with such ease and grace that I fooled myself into thinking I could do it too. Confession: I iron by throwing things back in the dryer. What made me think altar linens were my new specialty?

After 48 years of living with myself, I am still caught by surprise by the number of times I attempt to "help" when clearly the helpful thing is to stay far away. Haven't I learned where my gifts and talents do and do not lie by now? Giving something new a whirl, of course, can uncover hidden abilities and is very often a revealing and worthwhile thing to do. But when you, like me, have NEVER been able to do a craft project, the odds of creating magic with 250 little glass beads and a glue gun are not good.

My point? There are always a million and one opportunities to serve the Lord, and to serve one another, both here and out in the world. Many people I know have found special ways to use their unique gifts and talents. At church? Maybe as a Sunday School teacher or choir member. Out of church? Maybe as a soup kitchen volunteer, a Habitat for Humanity builder. Some are still wondering how to take the plunge and be a blessing in the world this year.

Here's my advice—think of what you already love to do, what you would happily do if you had a free day. Where your heart lies is where you should serve. There's no virtue, for anyone, in glumly plodding ahead in an area you dislike. Discernment, self-knowledge, is key. Would you, like me, prefer a lengthy prison sentence to hammering a nail? Would a dinner concocted in your kitchen more likely nourish, or poison, a new mother and family? Conversely, is gardening a passion? Or are yours the loving arms that can soothe fussy babies? As the Nike commercial says, then Just Do It. Pick up the phone. Send an email. Volunteer—enjoy the great feeling of work done for God's glory—and enrich the world by bringing your interest and enthusiasm to a ministry, in or out of church. Life together should be joyous and not onerous, so do what you love, and the rewards will come back to you a hundredfold.

I, meanwhile, will keep pouring my passion and focus into our congregational youth and family programs, our mission and outreach—and maybe an occasional skit.

By the way, Julie actually enjoys being on the altar guild and shows much more promise than me…anybody want to take over as her partner?

SUMMER TRAINING

"For day and night Your Hand was heavy on me; my strength was sapped as in the heat of summer."

--Psalm 32:4

I'm riding a SEPTA train on this scorching summer night, heading away from Suburban Station, Philadelphia, out towards Oreland. The car is nearly empty, so I am alone with my thoughts. Looking out the window, I have a sudden, vivid flashback.

Riding another SEPTA train on a stifling, long-ago July morning, headed to my "acting" job as a Kelly Girl. The temp service had been a godsend during previous career dry spells and was keeping me going now. Since Steve and I arrived in town, I had spent a stint in the echocardiogram department of the Medical College of Pennsylvania Hospital. There, I fantasized that I was a skilled technician, running life-saving tests on ailing hearts (I actually gave out the release forms to the anxious patients). Now, my role had shifted from medicine to law. I was subbing in the Morgan, Lewis and Bockius library in Center City. I had ample time to imagine myself as a brilliant young associate, prepping for a ground-breaking case (I actually helped check out books). I looked forward to the camaraderie of the librarians—but mostly to the air-conditioning. I eagerly anticipated my evening reunion with my husband. Steve would have his own tales to tell after a grueling day selling Time-Life books on the phone: "You're a master plumber? Well, that's great! But you'll still love Basic Plumbing for your home library. Just three easy payments of...Hello?"

Living in Philadelphia in the summer of 1980 was like dwelling in an oven. Getting up multiple times during the night to angle the box fan so the tepid air could blow even vaguely in the direction of our bed. Cool showers were exercises in futility, as we were instantly re-drenched in sweat. We subsisted on yogurt and salad, because heating the stove was unthinkable.

Many times during this sweltering month, Steve and I second-guessed ourselves. Was moving into an old Lincoln Drive apartment building the world's dumbest idea? We'd spent most of our three year marriage traveling, doing dinner theatre down South and children's theatre throughout the Northeast. We'd been footloose and furniture-free, eating cheap, tooling around in a decrepit Chevette. We joked that we finally ran out of gas in Philly and decided to stay put. Actor friends of ours scoffed: we were wimps for not renting a tiny roach-infested walk-up (and up and up and up) in Manhattan. But we felt we were making a "grown-up" decision to settle down where we might actually be able to build a life, have a family. Of COURSE we would still make all the big NYC tryouts—Broadway was just a train ride away, right?

The jam-packed car clattered down the track. I gazed through a hazy window as layers of city (slum, modest neighborhood, sleek high rise in the distance) flew by. I was 23 years old. When was life going to stop feeling like a rehearsal for something else? When was Philadelphia going to feel like a place where I belonged? We were clinging to our theatrical ambitions by our fingernails, hitting every local non-union call. I'd done a few voice-overs ("Head to Bellmawr Furniture's BIG BIG BIG clearance sale!!!") We were even doing community theatre, a series of unpaid gigs all over the area. Somehow, we were always too tired and broke to head North to the Big Apple. Philly might as well have been Topeka for all the good the proximity to New York did us.

I was still wrestling with all these questions and doubts as the train pulled into the station. The humidity was a wet smack in the face as I climbed the steps to the sidewalk. Each step taking me closer. Closer to being a real grownup. A Philadelphian, even. I joined the crowds rushing to work on streets I was coming to know well. Maybe, just maybe, we never would be Broadway stars. Maybe there were other, unimaginable, adventures awaiting us. Right here. And maybe, just maybe, that would be OK.

31 years later. We're still here. We've managed to raise five children on the income from our small theatre company. Our ambitions and our dreams have changed—we now wish for good health, safety for the kids, a paid-off mortgage. We've had

adventures—wonderful, tragic—unimagined that long-ago July morning.

Which brings me to this hot summer evening. I've been in Center City at a concert with my oldest son, an all-grown-up composer, and now I'm heading home. I've been a grownup myself for decades now. But as I gaze out the hazy train window, I can still see her—the young actress and wife from the summer of 1980. I remember every question, every doubt. Every dream. And I reach out a hand to touch hers against the glass. *It's another scorcher*, I whisper. *But it'll be OK.*

YOU'VE GOT A FRIEND

"…Winter, spring, summer or fall/all you've got to do is call/and I'll be there/you've got a friend…"

--Carole King

Check it out. I am closing in on 400, everyone.

Facebook Friends, that is.

Now I realize that, compared to the numbers my children have racked up (986, Julie? Really?) this is chump change, but I am thrilled in a Mom sort of way. My large-ish posse is mostly comprised of people I actually do know, for one thing. Oh, there's one guy I do NOT recall accepting a friend request from, but clearly I did. He has "liked" my status a couple of times and I am eager to unfriend this "friendly" stranger. But I can't figure out how to do that quite yet, and am too proud to ask my kids.

Anyway, my FB Friends and I enjoy going to the movies and shopping and on trips together, having long discussions over wine on the porch, sharing stories of our children and their antics. When one of us is sick, the other is at the door and at the ready with chicken soup, *People* magazine and sympathy. We tell each other our deepest secrets and know they will be kept; we would trust them with our very lives.

Ohhhhh, right. They're not those kinds of friends. My bad.

The word "friend" has undergone a sea change in recent years. Now, thanks to Mark Zuckerberg, it refers to any random person in (or out of) your life who has even the most marginal connection to you. What do they really know about you? Oh, they all know your birthday ("Have a great one!"). Your unfortunate addiction to Farmville. Your penchant for posting "hilarious" YouTube videos of babies, monkeys, baby monkeys, etc. For many in your ever-widening circle of chums, that's about all they know about you.

But what is a friend, in the classic sense of the word?

For starters, if you have more than a handful in a lifetime, you've hit the jackpot. A friend is in it with you forever, whether that be a brief span or from diapers to, well, diapers. Friends eat your kitchen experiments—deflated soufflés, charcoal briquettes that once were steaks— without complaint. They help you look on the bright side when the color you painted the entire house dries more SCREAMING PURPLE than Smoky Lilac. They drive you to scary doctor's appointments, and hold your hand for the test results. Real friends can speak truth to you with so much love that the truth is bearable. Friends like that are rare as black pearls, and need to be treasured as such.

We're not all that lucky at various stages of life. As our family relocated often, I gamely tried to become part of the "gang" at Epiphany School, and Our Lady of Perpetual Help School, and St. Jude School, and so on. In those days, as the eternal New Kid, I attracted the Mean Girls like a magnet. Peggy and Pam and Linda heaped scorn on my outfits, my hairstyle, my lisp. My Mom had similar pre-teen experiences, and so did my daughters. Ah, girlhood! Are we having fun yet?

It took three more family moves and three high schools before I found more than one lifelong friend, and a long time after that before my handful grew at all. Our wild and crazy theatre years provided lots of laughs with our eccentric fellow actors, but when the show closed, so, most often, did the relationships. By and large, that was just as well. Conversations with these buddies tended to revolve around themselves to a humorous degree ("But enough about me. What did YOU think of my performance?")

Cliché as it sounds, having children and joining a church were the keys to developing some of my very closest friendships. These folks are my "black pearls," and I treasure them beyond all telling.

Friendship was not a numbers game with Christ. He, with His boundless heart, embraced the whole world, but when it came to real intimacy, unequivocal trust and unspoken understanding—well, that was the province of a few special ones. And that model gives us permission to feel likewise. We are called to love everyone, but that doesn't mean we have to be intimately close to them all. By its deepest and most profound definition, friendship is the concentrated work of a lifetime, a meeting of minds and souls not often or easily replicated.

In this world of "more"—more things, more distractions, more casual connections—true friendship is an invitation to have "less." Less stress. Less worry. Less pretending. A chance to stand before the mirror of our friend's eyes, and accept, lovingly, the person we see reflected there. Friendship is powerful, powerful stuff. Life-changing stuff.

How rich our lives can be with such companions. So let's reclaim the word from the social network, shall we? I have 400 contacts who are on Facebook. I do not have 400 "friends" and, I'll wager, neither do you. Let's end this ridiculous numbers game. And when we find our true friends, then we can count ourselves among the blessed ones.

THE LUCKIEST

"Now I know all the wrong turns, the stumbles and falls
Brought me here
And where was I before the day that I first saw your lovely face?
Now I see it every day and I know that I am…the luckiest."

--Ben Folds

If a huge old tree falls across a yard, and there is someone right inside the house to listen, does it make a sound?

I now have an answer to that question.

Amazingly, not that much of a sound.

I was in the kitchen cooking dinner. Julie was asleep on the family room sofa, taking a Friday snooze after an exhausting week in school.

The only thing I heard was nothing very remarkable. Just a rustling of leaves, a sound like the wind whipping through the branches. Then a soft thud.

When I looked out the window, I saw it. The largest tree on our property had fallen over, completely uprooted. It had fallen away from the house, and taken down another big tree and a part of our neighbor's fence with it.

It's a mess out there, and it's going to be an expensive nuisance to deal with.

But we are the luckiest.

Because the sofa where Jules slept is right against a window. Right outside that window was the tree.

And had the tree fallen the other way, we might very well have lost our daughter.

Right after Christmas, Sheridan woke up in New York in the middle of the night with severe stomach pains. He is the family stoic, who as a child used to deal with intense pain by doing pushups…Sheridan: the musical equivalent of a Navy SEAL. Needless to say, he braved it for hours and hours (and hours). Finally, during the early afternoon, he took a cab to the ER at St. Luke's Hospital, where it was discovered that his appendix was about to rupture. He got there just in time.

He was the luckiest.

I often bemoan my bad fortune. It's been 40 years since I last won anything, and that was a cheap tote bag at the grand opening of an Atlanta drugstore. I consider every raffle ticket purchased to be an automatic donation to the cause, whatever it may be, because there's not a chance I'll ever see a prize of any sort. If the Publisher's Clearing House car ever rolls up to our driveway, it will only be to check directions to the home of a lucky friend.

But these two narrowly averted calamities reminded me. I'm not, after all, the Biggest Loser. Quite the opposite, in fact.

Counting your blessings is a cliché, but it is really the only counting that matters. We so often become experts at counting other things—shortcomings, grievances, what we miss, what we lack. On any given day, we can all enumerate many instances and areas where others are the winners, not us. Indeed, that kind of counting can become a regular rhythm, the beat running through our lives. Let's face it. Unless you are Bill Gates, someone else will always be able to trump your house, your car, your investment portfolio, your vacation spot. But look around. Stop and think. Can you walk, talk, see and hear? Do you have a roof over your head and food on your table? Did you wake up this morning? Do you have someone in this world who loves you? Do you have someone in this world to love?

Then you are the luckiest.

I look out the window and see the giant, felled maple tree. Realize how we came mere inches from tragedy. Know how many families do not have the incredible luck we have had all these years. Families who did absolutely nothing to deserve their bad fortune. Families who, legitimately, will have some questions for God when they get to Heaven. Questions I believe our loving God will be able to answer, as He wraps them in His arms, gifts them with their eternal reward.

Through the disappointments, financial struggles, and just plain downturns of everyday life, we are still the fortunate ones. For today at least, we've won the lottery.

Tonight, Steve and I count our Five Blessings, and pray for their continued safety, for their happiness. And for them to be able, every single day, to say, "I am the luckiest."

AND THE GREATEST OF THESE IS LOVE

"He that dwells in love, dwells in God. God is love. Therefore love."

--Henry Drummond

Boy, did I have a mental block about the Tooth Fairy!

Of the more than one hundred baby teeth tucked, ever hopefully, under five pillows over the years, I remembered the "choppers for dollars" swap exactly twice. Every other time, the kids had to wait and wait and WAIT for their cash. I was, in those days (and still am today!) both absent-minded and broke…a bad combination of traits for the magical sprite who made childhood wishes come true. When the little lost ivory nuggets would still be in their beds, unclaimed, on Morning #4, I had to do something. So I wrote the children notes, explaining and apologizing for my delay in rewarding them. These tiny missives, written in what I hoped looked like a pixie-hand, I signed, "Dentina." Dentina had been sick (the Fairy Flu). She had been busy collecting the 10,000,000 teeth lost just this week in China. She was sorry—here was a wrinkled dollar bill, with love!

What I didn't expect was that I would end up with five little pen pals. For every slip of paper Dentina left, I received a letter in return. To a child, they all thanked me for my belated largesse and accepted my apology. They also asked me about myself—where I lived (cloud? castle?), what I ate, how I traveled and what in the world I did with all those teeth.

I have no idea where the children's molars and incisors ended up—they are probably decaying somewhere in an unmarked envelope. What I do have are several entries from the Dentina Chronicles, and I wouldn't swap them for all the pearly whites in the world. For a few enchanted years, my kids and I participated in a gentle, harmless fantasy—that there was a mysterious someone out there who loved them, who counted and valued every single tooth in their heads.

I have a Santa story too.

One day when Sheridan was in 6th grade, I arrived home laden with Christmas presents that I was hoping to safely stash before everyone got home from school. As I turned the key in the lock, I heard Sher's voice. Oh, no! I'd totally forgotten that Sandy Run Middle School had early dismissal! He asked me what was in the bags—groceries, he hoped, because he was STARVING? At that instant I realized…we'd never had the Santa Claus talk. We'd been operating strictly on a don't ask/don't tell basis. Even the previous summer, when I'd tackled the Birds and Bees (Sher listening, red-faced, as he pretended to read the newspaper), the Jolly Old Guy hadn't come up.

I stood there for a moment. Would I spill the beans and ask him to help me hide the gifts? I mean, for heaven's sakes, he was 11 years old! But then…as my oldest, he was already grown-up in so many ways. Did I have to strip him of the last vestige of his childhood? I suddenly recalled my long-ago "plausible" explanation for Santa's chimney-less entry into my New York high-rise—he had keys! To the service elevator, and to Apartment 7-A, of course! I vividly recall wanting to believe, to have faith in a mysterious someone who loved me, and listened to all my heart's desires.

As it turned out, Sheridan had known for quite some time. He just hadn't wanted to hear the words from me, so he hadn't inquired. As he grabbed the bags to help me hide them in the guest room closet, he asked if he could eat Santa's cookies on Christmas Eve and then said, "You know, it'll be fun to help keep the secret from the little guys."

There are people in this world who would put God in the category of Mr. Claus and Dentina—a make-believe being we invent to soothe us. A buffer from the rough realities of life. A magical, mysterious Someone who gives us all good things, counts every tooth in our heads. We long for a God, so we wish Him into existence.

My God is more than a wish. I believe in a real God, who made this unimaginably vast universe (to me, believing that this exquisitely complex creation just sprang up randomly from nothing is a much harder idea to swallow). I believe with all my heart that God is both the miraculous source of all existence and an ongoing, guiding force in our lives. We can argue the details till the cows come home—to presume to completely "get" God is to limit Him to what we very limited beings can grasp. The final answers are out beyond a trillion stars, lie deep within the soul of a newborn baby. Religions attempt to define Him—sometimes vilifying other faiths' visions of the Almighty. The best of them, however, offer a common language of worship; they offer times and places and ways to feel God's presence, and structures where questions and doubts can be wrestled with and, above all, love can be shown.

So who is God? In a way, perhaps, the myths of the Tooth Fairy and St. Nick can point us in the right direction. Someone gave me the gift of Love. And that same Love inspires this mom to create a Dentina for her precious children; motivates an 11-year-old brother to keep a secret called Santa for his siblings.

I believe in a God who is pure Love.

Love: I can't see, or hear, or touch it. I don't always understand it. But it's the realest thing I know.

CPSIA information can be obtained at www.ICGtesting.com
Printed in the USA
BVOW012307221111

276670BV00001B/6/P